Legislative History

Research for the Interpretation of Laws

Gwendolyn B. Folsom

Fred B. Rothman & Co.
LITTLETON, COLORADO
1979

ISBN 0-8377-0532-0

REPRINTED BY ARRANGEMENT WITH
THE UNIVERSITY PRESS OF VIRGINIA

Legislative History

Research for the Interpretation of Laws

Gwendolyn B. Folsom

The University Press of Virginia
Charlottesville

THE UNIVERSITY PRESS OF VIRGINIA

First published 1972

The statute shall be taken . . . *ex mente legislatorum,* for that is chiefe to be considered, which, althoughe it varie in so muche that in maner so manie heades as there were, so many wittes; so manie statute makers, so many myndes; yet, notwithstandinge, certen notes there are by which a man maie knowe what it was. . . . And so, in our dayes, have those that were the penners & devisors of statutes bene the grettest lighte for exposicion of statutes.

From the earliest English treatise on statutory interpretation, probably written somewhat before 1572. Samuel E. Thorne, ed., *A Discourse upon the Exposicion & Understandinge of Statutes. With Sir Thomas Egerton's Additions,* 151-52 (Huntington Library, 1942).

Preface

Since this manual is intended primarily as introductory material for beginners, normally law students, it first touches upon the general nature of the subject (Part I) and the legislative process, national or state, from which it is derived (Part II) before dealing with the basic sources of information documenting that process (Part III) and the step-by-step method of research in federal legislative history (Part IV). Special or additional considerations with reference to federal tax laws, constitutional provisions, and treaties are the subject of Parts V, VI, and VII. Experienced lawyers, of course, will find at least Part II completely unnecessary. But beginners and nonlawyers should find them all informative in the order here presented.

Scholars in other fields -- such as government, history, and sociology in particular -- may of course also have need for recourse to legislative history for one purpose or another. While their objectives or points of view may be different from those of lawyers, still they may find it informative to know what courts and lawyers do with such materials, what parts are useful, the basic sources of information, and how to find them. But no attempt is made here to relate what follows to the special research problems of those disciplines.

This is not a hornbook. It is a listing of ideas and sources plus a description of routines useful in making a search for federal legislative history. Citations to court opinions in the preliminary parts, and occasionally elsewhere, are not meant to be exhaustive but only illustrative.

For their valuable comments and suggestions, acknowledgments are due to Professors Charles M. Davison, Carl McFarland, Richard A. Merrill, and Thomas R. White as well as to two students, Thomas J. Igoe, Jr., and James J. Tanous.

Contents

PART I

KINDS AND USES OF HISTORY OF LAWS

Legislative history is normally associated with statutes because of the nature of the process of the representative assemblies which make them. It has been used since the early days of the Republic, although sometimes questioned or qualified. It is to be distinguished from other usable kinds of history in legal studies such as general history of a political, social, or economic nature; legal history in the sense of the state of the law at a given point in time; and statutory history in the sense of the development of a text in the course of repeated enactments. Legislative history as the term is used in this manual relates to the explanations of the legislators themselves, or the documents officially used or made by them, in the course of making a specific law. These materials then become important in the reading or interpreting of the laws to which they relate.

Courts are primarily interested in this kind of legislative history only as it bears upon some issue of interpretation before them in litigation. How courts view and use such history is stressed in this manual because it is the courts, not the legal profession at large, which have made legislative history important, have added it to the texts and precedents which lawyers may be held accountable to know, and have also limited its sources and effects. Not only because courts have led the way to the use of legislative history but also because they have done so in litigation, lawyers may think of it in those terms and limit it to litigious situations. Thus a lawyer with a specific case under a statute which may or may not cover or exclude it will search the legislative history to discover whether, in the process of making it, the legislators expressed their intentions explicitly or impliedly with reference to such cases. However, lawyers who are brought into statutory fields which are new or new to them may also find such materials useful in the general reading and understanding of the basic laws under which they must advise or otherwise represent public and private interests apart from litigation they may be conducting. Those who are engaged in continuing representation in developing fields may find it necessary to keep abreast of current legislative activities or possibilities in minute detail. To that end they may cumulate extensive files and even libraries of releases, drafts, testimony, proposals, and bills long before such things as committee hearings or reports, or general debates, are officially published. Moreover, materials such as these are not always published by Congress and publication of any kind is either nonexistent or severely limited in the great majority of the states.

In any event, to be sure, the term "legislative history" may be taken or intended to mean different things in different legal settings or for different kinds of legal or professional problems. Moreover, it is somewhat unrealistic to speak of it apart from situations in which there are a particular piece or body of legislation, questions or fact problems in the nature of cases or possible controversies, and the applicability of more or less established institutional or legal principles respecting the interpretation of laws. On the other hand, there is need for some overview, definition, and specification of techniques as in other areas of the law. That, for law students in an introductory way, is the purpose of this manual.

Ordinarily, legislative history has reference to a statute, federal or state. It should be noted, however, that other species of legislation may also have legislative history. Debates and reports of constitutional conventions and commissions and of legislatures, for example, comprise the principal legislative history of constitutions and their revision or amendment.[1] Negotiations culminating in a treaty may be used in ascertaining its meaning.[2] The notes of a drafting committee may in effect form the legislative history of court-made rules of

---

1. For examples of judicial use of such materials in construing constitutional provisions see Cramer v. United States, 325 U.S. 1, 22-24 (1945); Missouri v. Illinois, 180 U.S. 208, 221-23 (1901); Yelle v. Bishop, 55 Wash. 2d 286, 347 P.2d 1081, 1084-86 (1959). For a critique of their use see Wofford, The Blinding Light: The Uses of History in Constitutional Interpretation, 31 U. Chicago L. Rev. 502 (1964). For a state court opinion taking the position that constitutional debates should not be given weight in construing a constitution see Bowers v. Pa. Labor Relations Bd., 402 Pa. 542, 167 A.2d 480, 487 (1961).

For a description of the sources of legislative history of the national Constitution see Part VI of this manual.

2. See Part VII *infra*.

civil procedure.[3] Even the regulation of an administrative agency may have a legislative history.[4]

In the early years of the nation the Supreme Court did not hesitate to resort to legislative history in construing the Constitution and statutes.[5] There followed a period during which it was reluctant to use any extrinsic aids.[6] But with the widened use of legislative regulation and the consequent increase in cases involving statutory interpretation, a trend toward more liberal use of such aids

---

3. See, e.g., use of such notes in Adickes v. S. H. Kress & Co., 398 U.S. 144, 159-60 (1970); State v. Jensen, 395 S.W.2d 143, 145 (Mo. 1965).

4. See, e.g., National Broadcasting Co. v. United States, 319 U.S. 190, 193-96, 225 (1943), in which the Court made use of the extensive agency proceedings culminating in promulgation of the Federal Communications Commission's chain broadcasting regulations; American Trucking Ass'ns v. United States, 344 U.S. 298, 306-08, 318-20 (1953), in which the Court used similar materials respecting the motor carrier regulations of the Interstate Commerce Commission in determining the validity of those regulations. Cf. Peters v. Hobby, 349 U.S. 331, 344 (1955), in which agency comments embodied in the report of a Presidential commission, as well as the report and recommendation of the latter, were used in construing the resulting Presidential executive order. The Wisconsin court has used as legislative history an explanatory letter from an agency transmitting its rule compilation to the state Revisor of Statutes. Loof v. Rural Mut. Cas. Ins. Co., 14 Wis. 2d 512, 111 N.W.2d 583 (1961).

5. From the beginning, references to the Federalist Papers were made in expounding the Constitution. E.g., Cohens v. Virginia, 19 U.S. (6 Wheat.) 264, 418-20 (1821).

6. What might be termed an intermediate or transitional position is that legislative history may not be used to determine the meaning of the words of a statute, but may be considered as reflecting light on its general purposes and the evils it sought to remedy. The Court took this view as to Congressional debates in such cases as Humphrey's Executor v. United States, 295 U.S. 602, 625 (1935). In an earlier case the Court stated that although the debates could not be used as a means of interpreting a statute, they could properly be used to ascertain the history of the period of its enactment. Standard Oil Co. v. United States, 221 U.S. 1, 50 (1910).

gradually developed.[7] In this respect American practice differs sharply from that of England.[8] Before the mid-point of the twentieth century, use of legislative history by the Supreme Court had become almost a matter of routine.[9] Thus in 1943 the Court rested a decision squarely on the ground that the court below erred in refusing to consider the legislative history of a revenue act.[10]

Use of legislative history by the state courts has come more slowly and is still much less extensive than in the federal courts. That would appear to be due, primarily, to the fact that in most states there is little available official documentation from which the legislative intent may be ascertained. The typical state publishes only the legislative journals, which show only the bare bones of legislative history--principally when and by whom a bill was introduced, to what committees referred and if reported favorably, what

---

7. See Frankfurter, Some Reflections on the Reading of Statutes, 47 Colum. L. Rev. 527, 542-543 (1947); Powell, Construction of Written Instruments, Part 3, 14 Ind. L.J. 309, 319-31 (1939).

8. In England, since the eighteenth century, legislative history may not be used. Theodore F. T. Plucknett, A Concise History of the Common Law, 335-36 (5th ed. 1956); see also Frankfurter, supra, 540-42; Powell, supra, 316-19.

9. See the citation of some 100 cases in the past decade, in which legislative history was said to be decisive in construction of a particular statutory provision, in Appendix A to dissenting opinion by Mr. Justice Frankfurter in Commissioner of Internal Revenue v. Church, 335 U.S. 632, 667, 687 (1949). For the Court's use of such materials in the succeeding years see Note, A Decade of Legislative History in the Supreme Court: 1950-1959, 46 Va. L. Rev. 1408 (1960).

10. Harrison v. Northern Trust Co., 317 U.S. 476 (1943).

amendments were introduced and adopted or rejected, the votes resulting in enactment or failure of passage, and the fact of approval or veto by the governor. As noted below, explanatory reports and debates are rarely published or otherwise available. To the extent that such materials exist, however, there is a growing tendency in state courts to resort to them.[11]

Experienced Congressional leaders today are aware of the significance of legislative history materials in statutory construction. They often take pains, in reports and in floor explanation of measures they sponsor, to spell out for that very purpose the intent of particular provisions. In some quarters it has been alleged that legislative intent is "manufactured" by deliberately drafting a statute in broad or ambiguous terms and then inserting in the committee report a statement giving the provision an interpretation which, if it had been plainly expressed in the statute, might not have been accepted by Congress.[12] In one recent instance, in-

11. See Part III infra. Some states have enacted statutes providing that courts may consider legislative history in determining the meaning of doubtful statutes. See, for example, Purdon's Pa. Stat. Ann. § 46-551 (1969), of general applicability; and Va. Code Ann. § 13.1-132 (1964), applicable to construction of the stock corporation law. Most such legislation, however, is merely declaratory of principles previously established by the courts and in any event is unlikely to have more than hortatory effect.

12. See Newman, A Legal Look at Congress and the State Legislatures, in Monrad G. Paulsen, ed., Legal Institutions Today and Tomorrow, 67, 76-77 (Columbia Law School Centennial Conference volume, 1959); Wasby, Legislative Materials as an Aid to Statutory Construction: A Caveat, 12 J. Pub. L. 262, 267-68; Cashman, Availability of Records of Legislative Debates, 24 Record of N.Y.C.B.A. 153, 154 (1969).

volving the Economic Stabilization program (wage-price control), legislative history was avowedly created in order to make clear that which, as a matter of procedure, the conferees deemed themselves precluded from expressly stating in the statute.[13] But normally such legislative history contains some useful and non-controversial expressions of general purpose as well as specific applicability. It is to be noted, however, that a great deal of what is said in committee reports and debates is merely a reiteration, paraphrase, or summary of the proposed legislation under discussion, which adds little or nothing to what the legislation already says on its face.

Professional literature of the past forty years is replete with argument over the propriety of the use of legislative history in statutory construction. Whether there is such a thing as a discoverable legislative intent has been questioned.[14] The controversy has centered principally over

---

13. In amending the Economic Stabilization Act of 1970 Congress desired to provide for the retroactive payment of wages agreed to prior to the wage freeze of midsummer 1971. But conference committees meeting to reconcile differences between Senate and House provisions are prohibited by the rules from inserting matter beyond the scope of provisions previously adopted by one or the other house. The conferees on the Stabilization Act therefore considered that they could not broaden the language of the provision in question. The phrase there used was "by law or contract" while the desire was to include wage increases previously "scheduled" or otherwise tacitly promised prior to the President's freeze order. This latter intent and the reason were candidly expressed in the conference report and spread upon the record in the House proceedings. 117 Cong. Rec. H12528 (daily ed., Dec. 14, 1971).

14. Radin, Statutory Interpretation, 43 Harv. L. Rev. 863 (1930); contra, Landis, A Note on "Statutory Interpretation," id. 886.

the relevance and competence of legislative history materials in ascertaining legislative intent as well as the weight which should be accorded them.[15] The Supreme Court not infrequently divides as to what is shown by or may be implied from legislative history.

A. The Usable Kinds of History

There are at least four or five very different kinds of history used in the interpretation of legislation. Each is distinguished by either the materials utilized, the objectives sought, or both. They may affect the approach to legislative research. They range from general to more and more specific materials and inquiries.

History of external events leading to the introduction and adoption of a law is often referred to by courts in determining the legislature's objectives. Material of that nature is sometimes referred to as the "history of the times."[16]

15. See Radin, A Short Way with Statutes, 56 Harv. L. Rev. 388, 410-11 (1942); Sparkman, Legislative History and the Interpretation of Laws, 2 Ala. L. Rev. 189 (1950); Breitel, The Courts and Lawmaking, in Paulsen, ed., supra note 12, at 1, 29-34; Stringham, Crystal Gazing: Legislative History in Action, 47 A.B.A.J. 466 (1961); and see also the references in note 12 supra. On the subject generally see de Sloovere, Extrinsic Aids in the Interpretation of Statutes, 88 U. Pa. L. Rev. 527 (1940); H. W. Jones, Extrinsic Aids in the Federal Courts, 25 Ia. L. Rev. 737 (1940); Nutting, The Relevance of Legislative Intention Established by Extrinsic Evidence, 20 B.U.L. Rev. 601 (1940).

16. United States v. Union Pacific R. Co., 91 U.S. 72, 79-83 (1875) (using "history of the times" giving rise to a statute granting financial aid to railroad). For other examples of use of such material see Inland Waterways Corp. v. Young, 309 U.S. 517, 520-22 (1940) (historical background of National Banking Act of 1864); Engel v. Vitale, 370 U.S. 421, 425-33 (1962) (establishment clause of First Amendment).

It has been used, for example, to justify a holding that a particular exercise of the police power is reasonable because of evils existing at the time of enactment.[17] For such purposes reference works on general or current history or events may be used and useful. Often the exploration of scientific or professional literature may be rewarding.[18] But such material merges with the gathering and presentation of factual data which, although of primary importance in litigation, is beyond the scope of this manual.

It is very often necessary to inquire into the prior state of the law generally on the subject at issue as background for the consideration of what changes, if any, were contemplated at the time of the adoption of legislation. This could be called "legal history." It is implicitly, if not expressly, involved in most interpretative problems, for what is actually new law depends upon ascertaining what the old law was. The former law may have taken the form of the previously existing legal order, the common law as found in precedent, or earlier legislation. This form of inquiry and research may take place, even where legislation is not being

---

17. E.g., Fried v. Kervick, 34 N.J. 68, 167 A.2d 380, 386-88 (1961), using the existence of economically disastrous "price wars" in upholding a statute prohibiting rebates on retail sales of gasoline.

18. A noteworthy example of the use of such materials was the famous "Brandeis Brief," which imported the consideration of relevant sociological studies into the consideration of the factual setting for legislation under constitutional attack. See Glueck, Law and the Stuff of Life, 14 Harv. L.S. Bull. 3 (1963).

interpreted, in order to discover the reason or nonreason for precedents preliminary to considering whether courts should adhere to them.[19] The research required for this purpose is, therefore, of a general legal nature and not within the scope of this manual.

Where legislation has been on the books over a period of time, it is sometimes informative to trace the chronological course of development of a specific provision during that period. An inquiry of that character may reveal, for example, that public policy has been consistent notwithstanding alterations of language, has developed by stages, or has shifted or reshifted course.[20] This might be called the "statutory" or the "code" history. It is frequently referred to in professional literature as the "history of the legislation." The materials of such research are mainly the laws as they read and appear on the face of the statute book over a period of time. For this purpose, references to the earlier laws are ordinarily available in abbreviated form in the derivation notes to the provision in annotated codes or compilations. But occasionally, although citing intervening

---

19. E.g., Moragne v. States Marine Lines, 398 U.S. 375 (1970).

20. E.g., Willingham v. Morgan, 395 U.S. 402, 405-07 (1969) (history of federal officer removal statute used to support a broad construction); Jarecki v. Searle & Co., 367 U.S. 303, 309-11 (1961) (tracing history of income tax provision respecting "discovery" as an aid to construction of a similar provision in excess profits tax act); American Airlines, Inc. v. Battle, 181 Va. 1, 8-12, 23 S.E.2d 796, 800-01 (1943) (using statutory history of gasoline tax act as well as its legislative history).

amendments, such codes refer merely to the last prior code -- which may make it necessary to resort to the prior code or codes in tracing the statutory history back to its beginnings.

The same sort of statutory history may also, or alternatively, involve the course of related legislation rather than the specific provision directly involved.[21] In this case the existence and history of related legislation may be obtained from various sources. Indexes to the federal statutes enacted during each session of Congress are contained in the individual volumes of the Statutes at Large. There are also general indexes covering the period through 1931.[22] But usually research will begin with the indexes to codes, from which references to current legislation on the same subject may be gleaned. The development and relation of the latter to the provision immediately involved must then be pursued as the problem at hand seems to require.

More important for present purposes is the legislative process of the federal and state legislative assemblies. In the course of that process there are opportunities for official and authoritative explanations of language in the course of the adoption of a specific measure or provision. That process usually begins after the introduction of

---

21. *E.g.*, United States v. Menasche, 348 U.S. 528, 532-535 (1955).

22. Middleton G. Beaman and A. K. McNamara, comps., Index Analysis of the Federal Statutes . . . 1789-1873 (Govt. Printing Office, 1911), and Walter H. McClenon and Wilfred C. Gilbert, Index to the Federal Statutes 1874-1931 (Govt. Printing Office, 1933). Both of these indexes cover only general and permanent laws.

a bill and ends either with its certification to the chief executive for signature or repassage over the latter's veto. Between these two events there may be hearings, committee reports, debates in full assembly, amendments and revisions, and mediation of differences between the two houses. Authoritative explanations of the purposes or meaning of the language of the resulting law during that period and incident to those processes comprise the "legislative history" as the term is normally used by courts and lawyers. It is in this sense that the phrase is used in this manual, the following pages of which deal with the materials and methods of research involved.

B. The Uses of Legislative History

The objective, then, of the usual legislative history search is to discover from authoritative sources the purpose or meaning of specific legislative language. In that respect it will be necessary to examine both (1) why or when interpretation, and hence legislative history, is called for and (2) what is to be taken into account. However, for completeness, it will help to mention first two special situations or variations.

Where the language of laws is general enough to permit it, courts may choose to limit or narrow their application in order to prevent unconstitutionality or to avoid serious problems of that nature.[23] In doing so, a court may wish to resort to the legislative history in order to determine the general legislative objective, to which, so far as that is constitutionally permissible, the terms or generalities in the law itself are then interpreted as being confined.[24] The use of legislative history for such a purpose differs from the ascertainment of legislative intent as to the meaning of specific words or phrases. The objective is different. The search is for the general legislative purpose. The latter, if suitable, is then used to rationalize a limitation upon otherwise general language appearing on the face of the law involved. But otherwise the materials and methods of research may be much the same as in seeking the legislative intent as to the meaning or application of specific words or phrases.

The other special situation is that in which interested persons desire to follow the legislative process while it is occurring with respect to a specific proposal which has not yet become a law. They may do this as lobbyists of course -- or as lawyers who are called upon to advise clients as to the effect upon their operations of the

---

23. A much cited precedent of this nature is The Abby Dodge, 223 U.S. 166 (1912), in which the Supreme Court limited the generality of the language of a federal law to accord with the territorial jurisdiction of Congress. Other examples are International Machinists v. Street, 367 U.S. 740, 765-68 (1961), and United States v. CIO, 335 U.S. 106, 115-24 (1948).

24. E.g., United States v. Harriss, 347 U.S. 612, 620-26 (1954), in which the Court limited the coverage of the Federal Regulation of Lobbying Act to lobbyists for pay in order to preserve the constitutional right of petition in others.

proposals or changes therein as they appear at the successive stages of an ongoing legislative process. This might be called the daily legislative history. It may involve oral as well as documentary approach or search. Because of the time factor, furthermore, it is not always practicable to await the usual slow distribution of officially printed documents and other relevant materials. In Congress the pursuit of such information is normally done on the spot by trade association and other group representatives. It may, of course, be done by lawyers for their clients or by individuals for themselves. But the wheels turn sufficiently slowly in Congress, and the Government Printing Office operates with sufficient dispatch, for many people to rely for such information on the variety of publications mentioned in the later parts of this manual. State legislatures, on the other hand, meet less continuously, for short periods, and may act with relative speed. There the same oral or on-the-spot approaches may be made. There are often special overnight publications or services which furnish their subscribers copies of bills and amendments as introduced or proposed along with other ascertainable actions as they occur. Important activities will of course be reported also in the local press. Generally speaking, however, only to a limited degree are the materials and methods described in the remainder of this manual available to the seeker after up-to-the-minute legislative history of pending bills in the federal and state legislatures.

Apart from such special situations, legislative history is used and useful in interpreting the scope or limitations of words used by representative assemblies in the laws they make. At least theoretically, the cardinal rule is that no resort may be had to legislative history unless the statute is ambiguous.[25] Stated another way, such materials may not be used to change the plain meaning of the statute. But language which appears plain on a cursory reading may, in its application to particular circumstances, give rise to ambiguity. And no matter how plain the language may seem, there is no reason why courts should not examine the legislative history as a precaution.[26] For example, the effect of a literal reading may conflict with the demonstrable purpose of the statute.[27] In any event, legislative history may not be used to "import an intent into legislation devoid

25. Ex parte Collett, 337 U.S. 55, 61 (1949). But in that case -- as in numerous others -- the Court after stating the rule proceeded to consider the legislative history in detail, finding it consistent with the plain meaning of the statute.

26. "But words are inexact tools at best and for that reason there is wisely no rule of law forbidding resort to explanatory legislative history no matter how 'clear the words may appear on "superficial examination."'" Harrison v. Northern Trust Co., 317 U.S. 476, 479 (1943). See also Association of Westinghouse Salaried Employees v. Westinghouse Elec. Corp., 348 U.S. 437, 444 (1955), wherein the legislative history was examined "to see whether that raises such doubts that the search for meaning should not be limited to the statute itself."

27. For example, in United States v. Public Utilities Commission, 345 U.S. 295, 312-15 (1953), the Court resorted to the legislative history of the Federal Power Act where a literal application of the statutory definitions would have excluded certain sales so as to thwart the statutory scheme.

of language fit to express it."[28] It has been said that, while courts are no longer confined to the statutory language, they are still confined by it.[29]

But Delphic pronouncements such as those should not obscure the central fact, which is that laws are no longer to be interpreted solely in the light of the language which appears in them. That development is in some measure a disavowal of the notion that laws are written to apprise or warn people of their content. Taken literally, it imposes on lawyers and other advisers an additional burden when they undertake statutory research. Such a search may require a completeness and scope of coverage not immediately apparent. This manifests itself in various ways. In the first place, all the relevant legislative history materials must be considered. It is well worth repeating that the total legislative history is to be considered rather than relying on iso-

---

28. Toll Gate Farms v. Milk Bd., 148 Conn. 341, 170 A.2d 883, 887 (1961). Such spurious use of legislative history has given rise to the quip that only when the legislative history is doubtful does one go to the statute. Frankfurter, Some Reflections on the Reading of Statutes, 47 Colum. L. Rev. 527, 543 (1947); Greenwood v. United States, 350 U.S. 366, 374 (1956). With what amounts to the addition of legislative history to the "written" law for interpretative purposes, argumentative techniques are multiplied. They may then be based not only on the text of the law or the explanations or applications in the legislative history but also, to the extent that neither is explicit, on the more general statements of purpose in either. In this situation the advocate will naturally stress text, history, or purpose accordingly as, in that order, they support his position. See Frederick B. Wiener, Briefing and Arguing Federal Appeals, 174 (Bur. of Nat. Affairs, 1967).

29. Frankfurter, supra note 28, at 543.

lated statements taken out of context.[30] In the second place, the whole of the statute, the prior legislation, and sometimes even later laws on the same subject may be pertinent and require examination of the respective legislative histories.

Thus, the legislative history of one provision of a bill may be helpful in construing another provision of the same bill.[31] When the legislative history search should extend to prior or subsequent legislative activities depends, of course, on the problem presented. Legislative history has been used to demonstrate that a statute, though a substantial reenactment of a prior measure, was intended to change the law.[32] But it may also be used to show that a later act, though in different language, was intended to continue earlier provisions unchanged.[33] The legislative history of a predecessor act, or of an earlier bill which failed of enactment, is also sometimes used as an aid to construction of a later act.[34] Or it may be used simply as historical perspective rather than as evincing the legisla-

---

30. Hust v. Moore-McCormack Lines, 328 U.S. 707, 733 (1946); Allen v. Board of Elections, 393 U.S. 544, 568-69 (1969).

31. Monroe v. Pape, 365 U.S. 167, 188-91 (1961).

32. Commissioner v. Bilder, 369 U.S. 499, 502-05 (1962); see also Ex parte Collett, 337 U.S. 55 (1949).

33. United States v. Dickerson, 310 U.S. 554 (1940).

34. United States v. Louisiana, 363 U.S. 1, 17 n.16 (1960); United States v. Plesha, 352 U.S. 202, 205-07 (1957).

tive intent of the later provision.[35] The legislative history of a later act may sometimes also be useful as a species of ex post facto legislative construction of an earlier one.[36] But the history of a later proposal which failed of enactment, although occasionally utilized,[37] is less persuasive because the failure to adopt the later proposal cannot usually be attributed to any one particular understanding of the meaning

---

35. Western P. R. Corp. v. Western P. R. Co., 345 U.S. 247, 251-54 (1953).

36. In Sioux Tribe of Indians v. United States, 316 U.S. 317, 329-30 (1942), the Court considered as virtually conclusive on the significance of one act a statement in a report on a pending bill made five years later by the same committee. In Galvan v. Press, 347 U.S. 522, 526-27 (1954), a memorandum inserted in the Congressional Record by the sponsor of a 1951 amendment to a 1950 act was considered to be a "weighty gloss" on the 1950 act. But debates on the War Labor Disputes Act could not be accepted as authoritative guides to construction of the Norris-LaGuardia Act, enacted eleven years earlier. United States v. United Mine Workers, 330 U.S. 258, 281-82 (1947). The Court has been reluctant to give effect to a congressional report on an appropriation bill as construction of the earlier statute stating an administrator's powers. Oklahoma Press Pub. Co. v. Walling, 327 U.S. 186, 197 (1946).

The legislative history of a statute implementing a recently adopted constitutional provision is sometimes used in a similar fashion in constitutional interpretation. See, e.g., Myers v. United States, 272 U.S. 52, 111-18 (1926), in which the Court used the legislative history of the act of the first Congress establishing the Department of Foreign Affairs in reaching the conclusion that the executive power of the President included the power to remove executive officers appointed by him with the advice and consent of the Senate.

37. E.g., Knight v. Employment Security Agency, 88 Idaho 262, 398 P.2d 643 (1965). See also Miner v. Atlass, 363 U.S. 641, 650-51 (1960), in which failure of the Court to adopt proposals to amend the General Admiralty Rules was given some effect in reaching a determination that a local court rule was inconsistent with the General Rules.

of the earlier act.[38] Where rejection indicates legislative acquiescence in administrative or judicial construction of the earlier statute, however, it is accorded weight.[39]

38. Wong Yang Sung v. McGrath, 339 U.S. 33, 47-48 (1950); State v. Glynn, 154 Conn. 237, 224 A.2d 711, 715 (1966); Kneeland v. Administrator, 138 Conn. 630, 88 A.2d 376 (1952); State v. Lancashire Fire Ins. Co., 66 Ark. 466, 51 S.W. 633 (1899). See also Flanagan v. Mount Eden General Hospital, 24 N.Y.2d 427, 248 N.E.2d 871, 874 (1969), refusing to give effect to failure of committee, with no reason given, to report out an amendatory bill but stating that, if the bill had been discussed in both houses and defeated, this would have constituted some indication of the legislature's purpose.

39. See, e.g., Zimmerman v. Wisconsin Electric Power Co., 38 Wis. 2d 626, 157 N.W.2d 648 (1968).

PART II

A BY-PRODUCT OF THE LEGISLATIVE PROCESS

A law student is likely to be only vaguely aware of the nature of the legislative processes of representative assemblies, federal and state. At best, the courses taken in law schools barely touch upon the basis, methods, and related by-products of the making of laws. One of the by-products--growing out of the methods of representative assemblies which in turn are based upon extensive constitutional provisions, traditions, and procedures rarely mentioned in courses on Constitutional Law -- is legislative history as the term is used in courts and in this manual.

The kinds and uses of such history have been the subject of Part I above. How it comes about and what makes it useful are interwoven with the nature and internal operations of legislatures. It is a subject on which there is a formidable literature. The technical and official sources for Congress alone include, in addition to the current rulebook for each house, Hinds' Precedents of the House of Representatives in eleven volumes to 1941 and Watkins and Riddick, Senate Procedure, S. Doc. No. 44, 88th Cong., 2d Sess. (1964).[40]

---

40. How Our Laws Are Made is a pamphlet of fifty pages or so issued on the general subject of legislative procedure in Congress, stressing the detail in the House of Representatives but including Senate procedure as well and concluding with a bibliography of official publications as well as illustrative

Secondary or unofficial sources which deal with the matter in one way or another are endless. However, for present purposes, what follows here deals with such matters only to the extent necessary to indicate why and how this form of history is produced. Detail and documentation are omitted both for purposes of brevity and to avoid obscuring the essentials. Furthermore, the operative system in Congress will be taken as the model both because it is the domestic prototype (all have common root in the old procedure of the British Parliament) and because the significant differences in state practice are easily noted. Five aspects should suffice for present purposes.

In the first place, the representative assemblies of nation and states must meet annually or, in some of the states, biennially. Since money bills run for only a biennium at most, there is always pressing business involving every subject requiring money from the public treasuries. Of course there is also much other business due to need or choice. Much of it cannot be accomplished in any one Congress or the life of any one state legislative assembly and hence must be carried over or revived in successors. For present purposes the point, however, is that the legislative mills grind on steadily and, in doing so, reflect to a considerable

---

forms of bills, reports, and completed (enrolled) laws. Originally written by Charles J. Zinn, it has been revised under the auspices of the House Committee on the Judiciary and issued as a House document at intervals of a year or two since 1953.

degree current needs, objectives, and accomplishments so far as the individual representatives or groups of representatives state them in one way or another apart from the strict text of the laws they make. The Constitution requires Congress to meet annually.[41] Hence there are new federal laws every year, each with its own particular legislative history.

There is one technicality in this respect, moreover, which affects the mechanics of official sources and hence the research routine. While legislatures are permanent institutions, each such national or state assembly has a limited life of its own. In other words, Congress is an ongoing body but a Congress is an assembly with a two-year life (its term being conditioned by the two-year term of members of the House of Representatives). Each particular Congress, consequently, is consecutively numbered beginning with the first and ending with the current one. For each particular Congress, moreover, there are two sessions (one for each year of its life) unless the President convenes it in special session "on extraordinary occasions."[42] Hence the documentary output of each Congress is identified by the number of the Congress and, usually, the session thereof also. While this makes for some ease of identification, it also produces

41. Art. I, § 4, and Amend. XX, § 2.

42. U.S. Const., Art. II, § 3.

complexities of research and citation when a legislative history runs beyond a single Congress.

In the second place, the members of a representative assembly all have a vote and hence a voice in the making of laws. It is not merely a matter of one-representative-one-vote but of each representative having more or less opportunity to express, in one way or another, his views as to his objectives, what he intends, and how he interprets the language of laws he is making. Since legislatures pride themselves as, and are customarily justified as being, deliberative assemblies, there must be some public give-and-take of a forensic nature. Therein there is much politics of course, but also a considerable stating of reasons and views as to what should be done, can be done, or is being attempted. The official recordation of such views becomes legislative history. Publication makes it usable. It is the lack of either recordation or publication in most of the states which makes this form of legislative history unavailable with respect to most state statutes. Some 500 vocal representatives in Congress, plus some recordation and publication of their intentions respecting important pieces of legislation, are bound to produce significant reading matter. Since it is narrowly confined to the texts under consideration, it might be called micro-history. History of a sort it nevertheless is, official and recorded. But where it is, how to find it, and the separation of the verbal wheat from the political chaff require understanding, skill, and knowledge of the actual workings of the legislative process in representative assemblies.

The third major factor, which has worked out to be of equal if not greater importance in this connection, is that (save for unicameral Nebraska) there are not one but two bodies of representatives in each American legislature. This means that the enacting process, at least so far as voting and debating goes, must take place twice (save for the making of treaties, in which only the Senate participates). But, as it has worked out, there is more than a doubling of this process because, when the two houses are not in perfect accord, a third operation becomes necessary in the form of some mediation between the two. In Congress it is accomplished by the appointment of mediators called "conference" committees consisting of principal participants from each house.[43] When such a group reaches agreement over differences respecting a piece of legislation, the conferees must communicate their solution and reasons to the houses they represent. These "conference reports" on which they collaborate and which they file thus become primary sources of legislative history.

Fourthly, and again of at least equal importance in many respects, is the participation of the executive branch. It is based on the veto power of the President.

---

43. The house which first approved a measure may, of course, agree to amendments made by the other house, in which event no conference is necessary.

(In the states, except North Carolina, governors also enjoy that privilege.) In this respect, although the function is not discussed in such terms, chief executives are actually a third house of the legislatures.[44] Moreover, because the President may refuse to agree to a law (and passage over such veto by a two-thirds vote of each house is difficult) the whole executive branch in effect participates in the statute-making process. Not only the President but also officers and agencies of the branch which he nominally heads both propose and object to legislation. Their views, particularly in opposition, are given much consideration because, presumably, they have the President's ear and may persuade him to veto any statute passed over their objections. The President's messages and agency communications thus become a significant part of the legislative history. Attempts to diagram the legislative process in Congress all illustrate a constant shuttling of bills back and forth between Congressional committees and the federal agencies concerned -- which is more of a problem for lobbyists than for scholars since, in the end, the written and published record discloses such nuggets of usable information as that sort of activity produces.

44. When the first Congress was enacting its first statute, it was urged in the Senate that the enacting clause should include the President in addition to the usual "Senate and House of Representatives ... in Congress assembled." But since the Constitution itself expressly referred only to the Congress with respect to the exercise of legislative powers generally (Art. I, § 1), the motion to list the President as well as the Senate and House of Representatives was defeated notwithstanding the support of Vice President John Adams. Journal of William Maclay ... 1789-1791, 15-16 (1927 ed.).

Lastly, there is the committee system.[45] Unlike the factors mentioned above, it is not mentioned in the federal Constitution (but may be in state constitutions).[46] It is the working arrangement by which a large assembly of representatives allocates its work, achieves some degree of specialization by groups, and channels the traffic through the legislative mill. The committees, in Woodrow Wilson's phrase, are the "little legislatures" in a national legislature which is "conglomerate, not homogeneous."[47] Apart from the participation of the general membership in the necessarily limited debates or proceedings on the floor of either house, open to all members of the house involved, the committees play the preeminent role in legislating and consequently in the making of legislative history. "There is one principle which runs through every stage of procedure," said Wilson nearly a hundred years ago, "the principle that

---

45. For a modern study of the operation of the committee system in Congress see George Goodwin, Jr., The Little Legislatures: Committees of Congress (U. of Mass. Press, 1970). For the historical development of the committee report system, and the utilization of reports in the legislative process, see Broden, Congressional Committee Reports, 33 Notre Dame Law. 209 (1958). There are also a number of works devoted to particular committees, some of which are noted below.

46. Committees were utilized by the British Parliament and the colonial assemblies. Congress has used them since the beginning of the federal government. Jefferson made provision for them in his Manual for the procedure of the Senate, which is still carried in the Senate rulebook.

47. Woodrow Wilson, Congressional Government, 113 (Houghton Mifflin Co., 1913; first published 1885).

the Committees shall rule without let or hindrance."[48] This they do by their hearings, by their reports sending bills to the house for action by the general membership, and by the statements of their chairmen, subcommittee chairmen, or members-in-charge during subsequent general proceedings of the house.[49] (Conference committees, as noted above, triplicate that function where there is a substantial disagreement between the houses.) Thus hearings, committee reports, and the statements of committeemen in such general debate as may be allowed become the primary sources of authoritative legislative history -- all of which are more particularly described in the next part of this manual.

While some Congressional hearings are in the nature of general investigations, most are held for the purpose of ascertaining or confirming the desirability of enactment of a particular bill, or group of related bills, after introduction and reference to the committee. Hearings may be conducted by the entire committee or by a subcommittee. They are not

---

48. Id. 74. Bills of course may also be buried in committee and thus produce no affirmative legislative history. "As a rule, a bill committed is a bill doomed," said Wilson one-sidedly in the book which brought him fame. "When it goes from the clerk's desk to a committee-room it crosses a parliamentary bridge of sighs to dim dungeons of silence whence it will never return." Id. 69.

49. Note, however, that the full dress proceedings on the floor of either house may be mere formalities at times, or in part. "The House sits, not for serious discussion, but to sanction the conclusions of its Committees as rapidly as possible," said Wilson in the book mentioned above, "so that it is not far from the truth to say that Congress in session is Congress on public exhibition, whilst Congress in its committee-rooms is Congress at work." Id. 79 and see also 102 et seq.

trials in any sense of the word. They are occasions for the oral airing of views to be sure, but they are not of the truly open or town-meeting type. Government representatives, when agencies are interested or available, are likely to make important general statements. Major economic or other interests may be allowed to speak. Individuals may be allowed to file statements. What is sometimes called the "lunatic fringe" may be discouraged or turned away. So far as such hearings are recorded and published they become at best a source of background or tertiary legislative history.

For generations the sheer bulk of legislative business has been deemed to make it necessary for each house of Congress to delegate to committees the major part of its day-to-day work in determining what laws are needed and what form they should take. Every bill or joint resolution, immediately after introduction, is therefore referred to a committee, and the house normally takes no action on the measure unless and until the committee reports favorably thereon. The primary function of the committee report is to inform the house to which the committee reports -- to apprise that body of the substance of the committee's recommendations and its reasons therefor. To the extent that the house passes the provisions as recommended by the committee, it is considered to have adopted as its own the views stated in the report. These reports, supplemented by any statements made by the committee-affiliated members in subsequent general proceedings of either house, become the heart of what is called legislative history, although other official documents or publications growing out of the legislative process may lend perspective or furnish background.

PART III

THE ACCEPTABLE SOURCES OF INFORMATION

Not all the verbiage nor all the maneuvers which attend the legislative process are regarded as relevant sources of legislative history as the term is used in federal courts. Consequently, research time may be used to best advantage by concentrating on the materials deemed acceptable or persuasive in that connection. With few exceptions, such history is limited to official documents in and of the legislative branch. For that purpose committee reports and related documents are the preeminent sources. Next are the statements of legislator sponsors of the legislation, usually the committeemen, in the proceedings open to all members of the house involved. But legislative history of any kind, it must be remembered, is a secondary source. Some of it is even less persuasive and of less utility than committee reports and the statements of committeemen in open house proceedings. So hearings--which usually precede such reports and proceedings but may be published later--are not only more difficult to find, procure, and use but also of comparatively slight utility. Amendments, executive messages, and the silence of senators or representatives when they might be expected to speak may also be involved in one way or another in court discussions of legislative history--but they are less intimately related to the process of assemblies and hence of less weight in court.

A. Official Documents or Submittals

With some historic (but virtually no other) exceptions, legislative history may be established only by the formal records of the proceedings and other official documents of the legislative body.[50] These may be supplemented in some instances from other official sources such as executive reports or statements. Testimony of individual legislators as to legislative intent--even of committee members and sponsors of the bills in question--is inadmissible.[51]

---

50. There are notable exceptions to this rule with respect to early federal materials. For the judicial practice of resorting to unofficial sources respecting the adoption of the Constitution, see Part VI below. A similar practice developed with respect to the early proceedings of the Senate, whether comprising legislative history of statutes or of constitutional amendments. Until 1794 the Senate sat behind closed doors, and its debates were not officially recorded. For its proceedings during that period the Supreme Court has not hesitated to supplement the Annals of Congress and the Senate Journal by resort to private records and correspondence. The principal such source is the Journal of William Maclay, United States Senator from Pennsylvania, 1789-1791, edited by Edgar S. Maclay. Maclay's journal remained in the possession of his family for over a century; portions were privately printed in 1880 under the title Sketches of Debate in the First Senate of the United States, in 1789-90-91. The first complete publication appeared in 1890; an edition with introduction by Charles A. Beard, published in 1927 by A. and C. Boni, was reprinted in 1965 by F. Ungar Pub. Co. John Adams' diary and letters of James Madison have also been used for this purpose. See, e.g., Williams v. Florida, 399 U.S. 78, 93-97 (1970); Myers v. United States, 272 U.S. 52, 115 (1926).

51. For a classic illustration of this rule see City of Spokane v. State, 198 Wash. 682, 89 P.2d 826 (1939), refusing to allow proof of legislative intent by affidavits of some 100 members of the legislature, and depositions of the governor and chairmen of the legislative committees. See

Even as to unreported hearings of state legislative committees, testimony of witnesses as to sponsors' statements is inadmissible.[52]

Occasionally, however, a report or other document of a non-Congressional federal agency, or even of a private organization, may form a vital link in the chain of legislative history respecting a particular statute. Thus recommendations of executive departments for, against, or suggesting changes in proposed legislation will frequently be reproduced in the legislative hearings or committee reports. Or the latter may simply state that a particular provision was added on the recommendation of the Judicial Conference or of the American Law Institute,

---

also Epstein v. Resor, 296 F. Supp. 214, 216 (N.D. Cal. 1969) (affidavit of Congressional sponsor); Nat'l School of Aeronautics v. United States, 142 F. Supp. 933, 938-39 (C. Cls. 1956) (Senate subcommittee chairman); Board of Education v. Presque Isle County Bd. of Ed., 364 Mich. 605, 111 N.W.2d 853 (1961) (individual legislator); Wiseman v. Madison Cadillac Co., 191 Ark. 1021, 88 S.W.2d 1007 (1935) (committee member); Rausch v. Nelson, 134 N.W.2d 519 (N.Dak. 1965) (member of code revision commission as to commission's intent). The California court, however, in reading corrections of "technical errors" into a reapportionment measure, utilized affidavits of legislative employees who participated in drafting the act. Silver v. Brown, 48 Cal. Rptr. 609, 409 P.2d 689 (1966). And a lower New York court recently relied heavily on a letter from a member of the legislative subcommittee which drafted and sponsored a statute. In re John Children, 61 Misc. 2d 347, 306 N.Y.S. 2d 797, 808-10 (1969). See also Yelle v. Bishop, 55 Wash. 2d 286, 347 P.2d 1081, 1084 (1959), in which newspaper report of constitutional convention proceedings was utilized in absence of complete official report.

52. Peery v. Board of Funeral Directors, 203 Va. 161, 123 S.E.2d 94 (1961). See also Third District Land Co. v. Toka, 170 So. 793 (La. App. 1936).

in which event it may be necessary to consult the text of that recommendation.

B. Committee Reports and Related Documents

Ordinarily the most persuasive element of legislative history is the report of the legislative committee recommending its enactment "A committee report represents the considered and collective understanding of those Congressmen involved in drafting and studying proposed legislation" and hence may be of greater weight than random statements made in floor debates.[53] But sometimes there are unusual circumstances resulting in judicial acceptance of a debate statement in preference to a conflicting statement in a report.[54] On the other hand, matters may be discussed in debate which are not touched on in the committee reports. Where the language in issue has been the subject of difference between measures approved by the two houses and then reconciled in conference, the conference report will be most important.[55]

In state legislatures, formal committee reports are not routinely made. To the extent that they are available, the

53. Zuber v. Allen, 396 U.S. 168, 186 (1969).

54. *E.g.*, Chicago, M., St. P. & P. R. Co. v. Acme Fast Freight, 336 U.S. 465, 473-76 (1949), wherein the Court gave more weight to an explanation of a provision in a pending bill, made in the House debates by a member of the committee which drafted it and unchallenged on the House floor, than to a flat statement to the contrary in the House committee report which had not been submitted to committee members.

55. See Commissioner v. Acker, 361 U.S. 87, 94 (1959) (dissenting opinion); Leedom v. International Union, 352 U.S. 145, 149-50 (1956).

state courts now tend to permit their use as an aid to statutory construction.[56]

Reports of law revision commissions, and other reports made to or for a legislative body by special commissions, legislative councils, or other official agencies are given much the same effect with respect to legislation proposed by them as legislative committee reports, particularly where the legislative history proper makes plain that the legislature relied on such reports.[57] (For executive messages of similar nature, see below) Of particular importance to lawyers and law students are the explanations of advisory committees as to the language and purposes of rules of procedure promulgated by the Supreme Court for the federal district courts and by state supreme courts for inferior state courts.[58].

C. Statements of Sponsors in Proceedings of the Full House

Next in importance to committee reports are the statements of the sponsors of proposed legislation made in

---

56. State v. Chase, 224 Ore. 112, 355 P.2d 631 (1960); Mullis v. Celanese Corp., 234 S.C. 380, 108 S.E.2d 547 (1959).

57. Affronti v. United States, 350 U.S. 79, 82 (1955) (Criminal Code revision); Ex parte Collett, 337 U.S. 55 (1949) (Judicial Code revision); Conn. Rural Roads Imp. Ass'n v. Hurley, 124 Conn. 20, 197 A. 90 (1938); Harris v. Shanahan, 192 Kan. 629, 390 P.2d 772 (1964); Hohreiter v. Garrison, 81 Cal. App. 2d 384, 184 P.2d 323, 329-31 (1947); In re Martin's Estate, 365 Pa. 280 74 A.2d 120 (1950).

58. The Advisory Committee notes are even published in the United States Code as annotations to the Supreme Court's rules of civil and criminal procedure for the United States district courts. The same is true of the typical state compilation of similarly promulgated rules.

the proceedings or debates of the full legislative body. Language may be found in some court opinions to the effect that statements there made at best merely reflect the understanding of individual legislators.[59] But, where pertinent, they are almost routinely used by the federal courts.[60] Statements of sponsors in the house in which the provision originated are said to be of greater weight than those of supporters in the other house.[61] Where a provision takes final form in conference, the explanations of the conferees in presenting the conference report are highly persuasive.[62]

The views of opponents in debates and minority reports, since they may tend to overstate the reach of the provision opposed, are given little probative effect as against the stated views, or even silence, of proponents.[63] They may, however, be relevant and useful particularly when the

---

59. Zuber v. Allen, 396 U.S. 168, 186 (1969).

60. See, *e.g.*, Mitchell v. Kentucky Finance Co., 359 U.S. 290 (1959); United States v. International Union, 352 U.S. 567, 585-87 (1957); United States v. Wrightwood Dairy Co., 315 U.S. 110, 125 (1942).

61. Steiner v. Mitchell, 350 U.S. 247, 254 (1956); United States v. McKesson & Robbins, 351 U.S. 305, 313-14 (1956).

62. See, *e.g.*, Leedom v. International Union, 352 U.S. 145, 149-50 (1956); Brotherhood of Maintenance of Way Employees v. United States, 366 U.S. 169, 175 (1961); District of Columbia v. Murphy, 314 U.S. 441, 450-52 (1941).

63. National Woodwork Mfrs. Ass'n v. NLRB, 386 U.S. 612, 639-40 (1967); NLRB v. Fruit & Vegetable Packers, 377 U.S. 58, 66 (1964); Mastro Plastics Corp. v. NLRB, 350 U.S. 270, 288 (1956); Schwegmann Bros. v. Calvert Distillers Corp., 341 U.S. 384, 394-95 (1951).

proponents do not respond to a specific objection.[64] They may also add cumulative effect where both sides agree on the purpose and effect of a proposed provision.[65]

Statements of individual members of Congress inserted in the Congressional Record after passage of an act have been given no effect since they could represent only the personal views of those members.[66]

In most states legislative debates are not recorded, and in some states they are recorded but not published.[67] In the few states where the debates are available the state courts take varying views of their use. They are considered irrelevant in Pennsylvania.[68] In Connecticut they may be used. The Connecticut court considers a statement made in debate by the chairman of the sponsoring committee to be in the nature of a supplemental report to the legislature.[69] In New Jersey, where debates are not published, resort may be had to the sponsor's statement

---

64. Arizona v. California, 373 U.S. 546, 583 n.85 (1963).

65. United States v. Dickerson, 310 U.S. 554, 557-61 (1940). Opponents' views stated in hearings may also be so used. Brotherhood of Railroad Trainmen v. Chicago, R. & I. R. Co., 353 U.S. 30, 39 (1957).

66. National Woodwork Mfrs. Ass'n v. NLRB, 386 U.S. 612, 639 n. 34 (1967).

67. See Cashman, Availability of Records of Legislative Debates, 24 Record of N.Y.C.B.A. 153, 154-58 (1969).

68. Commonwealth v. Alcoa Properties, 440 Pa. 42, 269 A.2d 748 (1970).

69. Harris v. Planning Comm'n, 151 Conn. 95, 193A.2d 499 (1963); Bird v. Plunkett, 139 Conn. 491, 95 A.2d 71, 77 (1953).

accompanying the bill when introduced.[70]

D. Hearings Held by Committees

Congressional committee hearings are of limited utility as an aid to statutory construction.[71] They are used chiefly for background purposes or to corroborate a construction supported by other, more persuasive, materials. But where administrators participate in drafting and actively sponsor the particular provision being interpreted, their hearing presentations are accorded some weight.[72] Written presentations have been said to be less persuasive than oral ones.[73]

Since state legislative committee hearings are seldom reported, questions rarely arise as to their use.[74]

---

70. Deaney v. Linen Thread Co., 19 N.J. 578, 118 A.2d 28 (1955).

71. For criticism of the efficacy of the legislative hearing as a fact-finding process see Cohen, Towards Realism in Legisprudence, 59 Yale L.J. 886, 889-94 (1950). For its limitations as reflecting legislative intent see Wasby, Legislative Materials as an Aid to Statutory Construction: A Caveat, 12 J. Pub. L. 262, 271-73 (1963).

72. See Shapiro v. United States, 335 U.S. 1, 12 n.13 (1948); Zuber v. Allen, 396 U.S. 168, 192 (1969).

73. In Guessefeldt v. McGrath, 342 U.S. 308, 317 (1952), the Court considered written statements less likely to have had impact on the committee members or to reflect their views. Note, however, that Congressional committees customarily require witnesses to file written statements in advance and to limit their oral presentations to brief summaries. How Our Laws Are Made, H.R. Doc. No. 144, 92d Cong., 1st Sess. 13 (1971). Senate committees are directed by statute to impose the first requirement. 2 U.S.C. § 190a-1(c) (1970).

74. The Minnesota court has utilized hearings, from reporter's notes, without ruling directly on their competence to indicate legislative intent. Knopp v. Gutterman, 258 Minn. 33, 102 N.W.2d 689 (1960). The Connecticut court takes the position that hearing statements are not admissible as

E. Amendments Adopted or Rejected

Adoption or rejection of amendments to a pending bill may be critical, but it is difficult to generalize as to the effect of such action on statutory construction. The Supreme Court has on occasion reinforced its construction by resort to the fact than an amendment or substitute was adopted,[75] particularly when the amendment deleted a specific provision to a contrary effect.[76] But it has also refused to accept construction based on committee changes made without explanation--"mute intermediate legislative maneuvers."[77] Similarly, it has given weight to the fact that the legislative body considered and rejected an amendment;[78] but it has also stated that failure of a committee to adopt an unnecessary and superfluous amendment was of little significance.[79] Perhaps the best statement respecting the proper use of such

---

proof of legislative intent because it is impossible to determine what effect the individual discussion had upon the legislative action; and they do not become competent for consideration by inclusion in the arguments of a brief. Charlton Press v. Sullivan, 153 Conn. 103, 214 A.2d 354 (1965).

75. Blau v. Lehman, 368 U.S. 403, 411-12 (1962); United States v. Universal C.I.T. Credit Corp., 344 U.S. 218, 222-24 (1952); United States v. Local 807, 315 U.S. 521, 528-30 (1942).

76. Alaska v. American Can Co., 358 U.S. 224, 226-27 (1959); Carey v. Donohue, 240 U.S. 430, 436-37 (1916).

77. Trailmobile Co. v. Whirls, 331 U.S. 40, 60-61 (1947). See also Gemsco v. Walling, 324 U.S. 244, 260-61, 263-65 (1945).

78. Fox v. Standard Oil Co., 294 U.S. 87, 96 (1935).

79. Nishikawa v. Dulles, 356 U.S. 129, 135 n.8 (1958).

a legislative action is that it is, though not conclusive, "a circumstance to be weighed along with others when choice is nicely balanced."[80]

In the states, even though (or perhaps because) explanation in reports or debates is rarely available, amendments during the course of passage are frequently utilized.[81] Rejection of an amendment, however, may form a less reliable support.[82]

F. Relevant Executive Messages

Executive messages recommending enactment of legislation are one component of the legislative history of the resulting enactment. They normally appear or are quoted in published hearings, committee reports, and house proceedings. But messages or statements of the Executive accompanying approval of an action, while some-

---

80. Fox v. Standard Oil Co., supra, 294 U.S. at 96. On the significance of legislative inaction generally see Breitel, The Courts and Lawmaking, in Monrad G. Paulsen, ed., Legal Institutions Today and Tomorrow, 1, 11-15, 25-26 (Columbia Law School Centennial Conference volume, 1959); and Hart, Comment, id. 40, 45-47.

81. Industrial Commission v. Milka, 159 Colo. 114, 410 P.2d 181 (1966); Rossiter v. Whitpain, 404 Pa. 201, 170 A.2d 586 (1961); Morris v. State, 271 Ala. 290, 122 So. 2d 914 (1960); Gilbertson v. McLean, 216 Ore. 629, 341 P.2d 139, 145-46 (1959); American Airlines v. Battle, 181 Va. 1, 23 S.E.2d 796 (1943).

82. See, e.g., Board of Education v. N.J. Education Ass'n, 53 N.J. 29, 247 A.2d 867, 877-78 (1968), taking the position that the fact that the legislature overrode a conditional veto and refused to adopt an amendment proposed by the governor does not suggest that the legislature intended the implication the governor sought to foreclose.

times used as indicating legislative intent,[83] are perhaps more properly considered as contemporaneous executive construction rather than as a part of the legislative history proper. Veto messages are frequently pertinent with respect to later legislative action on the same subject.[84]

G. Apparent Silence or Inaction

Absence of discussion of an issue in the legislative materials may be less decisive than other legislative history.[85] But sometimes it is a factor in statutory construction.[86] The silence of sponsors may be "pregnant with significance," particularly where some striking change is claimed without support in the legislative history.[87] Ambiguous or inexplicit legislative history may simply be used as not contradicting the court's reading of the

---

83. E.g., State ex rel. Coleman v. Kelly, 71 Kan. 811, 81 P.450, 454-57 (1905), in which the governor's message accompanying approval of an act was used to support the holding that it was intended to provide for a work of internal improvement and hence invalid under the state constitution. See also Harris v. Shanahan, 192 Kan. 629, 390 P.2d 772 (1964).

84. See, e.g., Wong Yang Sung v. McGrath, 339 U.S. 33, 39 (1950); but see note 82 supra.

85. Vermilya-Brown Co. v. Connell, 335 U.S. 377, 385 (1948).

86. Benz v. Compania Naviera Hidalgo, 353 U.S. 138, 144 (1957); United States v. American Trucking Ass'ns, 310 U.S. 534, 546-48 (1940).

87. NLRB v. Fruit & Vegetable Packers, 377 U.S. 58, 66-67 (1964); see also National Woodwork Mfrs. Ass'n v. NLRB, 386 U.S. 612, 640 (1967); Rewis v. United States, 401 U.S. 808, 811-12 (1971).

statute.[88] Lack of opposition and speed of enactment have sometimes been used to support construction of a measure as not intended to cover controversial matters.[89] The same is true of a codification bill as not intended to make substantive changes.[90] Absence of controversy as to one provision may be given special significance by contrast with heated debates on other provisions of the same bill.[91]

---

88. Ladner v. United States, 358 U.S. 169, 174-76 (1958); Prince v. United States, 352 U.S. 322, 328 (1957); Western Union Tel. Co. v. Lenroot, 323 U.S. 490, 498-501 (1945).

89. United States v. Central Eureka Mining Co., 357 U.S. 155, 165 (1958).

90. Trustees of Schools, etc. v. Sons, 27 Ill. 2d 63, 187 N.E.2d 673 (1963).

91. Adickes v. S. H. Kress & Co., 398 U.S. 144, 164-66 (1970).

PART IV

FINDING GUIDE TO RELEVANT FEDERAL MATERIALS

Despite substantial legal literature on the use of legislative history and extensive references to it in court opinions, slight information is available in published form as to how and where to find it.[92] For federal statutes, what is usually a laborious search may be simplified as well as accurate if the requisite routine is followed in an orderly manner. The steps vary somewhat according to the date of enactment of the particular statute involved. With respect to any statute, however, the essential elements are four or five in the following order of importance: (A) Know the few critical types of official source publications. (B) Get the bill, Congress, and statute numbers for the particular subject at hand. (C) Find and examine both House and Senate committee reports as well as any conference reports. (D) Check the proceedings of each house and read the explanation

92. The sources of the legislative history of federal statutes, and officially published research aids, are described in detail in Laurence F. Schmeckebier and Roy B. Eastin, Government Publications and Their Use, Ch. 6 (2d rev. ed. 1969); see also Emerson and Fuller, How to Find and Use Federal Legislative Materials, 51 W. Va. L. Q. 169 (1949); Finley, Crystal Gazing: The Problem of Legislative History, 45 A.B.A.J. 1281 (1959). No article has been found specifically addressed to finding legislative history of private federal acts. But helpful information as to the detail of congressional procedures for handling private bills is contained in Note, Private Bills in Congress, 79 Harv. L. Rev. 1684 (1966). As to state statutes, see Cashman, Availability of Records of Legislative Debates, 24 Record of N.Y.C.B.A. 153 (1969). There are also occasional articles respecting materials available in a particular jurisdiction, e.g., Dana, Background Materials for Statutory Interpretation in New York, 14 Record of N.Y.C.B.A. 80 (1959).

and debates therein. (E) Examine the hearings and any other allied materials such as those previously mentioned in Part III. The first two of these -- the publications and particular identification numbers -- are preparatory. Therewith the researcher seeks relevant materials in the form of committee reports, house proceedings, and hearings or other background materials. In the actual working out of a legislative history, data respecting the reports, proceedings, and other materials tend to run together because they are interspersed in the official documentation. The legal craftsman must note them all as he scans the records.

A. The Essential Official Publications

Any statement of the step-by-step routine required to get at the necessary legislative history materials would be either obscure or frustrating without prior understanding of the principal basic documentary sources and publications. These, and some standard guides and supplementary compilations, are listed below with brief descriptions or references to more detailed information in this manual.

Bill. A written (printed) version of the text of a proposed law, as introduced in one or the other house of Congress by the member or members who sponsor it, is called a bill until it has been passed by the two houses and either approved by the President, not vetoed within the period fixed by the Constitution, or passed again over his veto. Proposed legislation is sometimes introduced in Congress as a joint resolution instead of a bill. The legislative process by which such resolutions may become law does not differ from that applicable to bills, and the term "bill" as used in this manual includes joint resolutions as well unless otherwise indicated.

Bills in each body, as well as each of the various types of resolutions, have for many years been given consecutive numbering for each Congress so that a measure introduced in the first session retains the number assigned it on introduction through all sessions of that same Congress. The first bill introduced in each of the two houses in the 92d Congress will be designated respectively S. 1 and H.R. 1 (and the first joint resolutions S.J. Res. 1 and H.J. Res. 1). The customary citation is S. 1, 92d Cong., 1st Sess.

Bills are printed and reprinted at various stages of the legislative process -- *i.e.*, on introduction (introduced print), as referred to committee (referred print), as reported by committee (reported print), as passed by one house (engrossed bill but captioned as "an act" of that house), and as passed in identical form by both houses (enrolled bill) for signature by the presiding officers of each house and by the President. The enrolled bill, when duly signed by all three, is *the* one final and official version, of which other official printings and publications are but presumptively correct copies. Amendments are also sometimes printed separately for the consideration of the house in which they are proposed.

Calendars. Both the Senate and the House regularly print for the use of their members calendars of pending business. Both are available in depository libraries. The Calendars of the United States House of Representatives and History of Legislation, usually referred to as the House Calendar, has a wider scope and contains more detail as to the history of bills than the Senate's Calendar of Business. The House Calendar is published daily while Congress is in session. It contains, in addition to various other listings, a table listing in order by bill or resolution number all bills and resolutions of the current Congress which have been passed by or reported to either house. For each such measure, it indicates the date of each action taken and the report numbers of committee reports. The final issue for each Congress also contains a list of bills with respect to which the President exercised a pocket veto.

Calendars of pending business are also printed by various standing committees of both houses for the use of committee members. The committee calendars contain data respecting hearings and other committee action not included in the calendars of their parent bodies. They are, however, not widely available.

Committee reports. When a committee of Congress desires to recommend action by its parent house, it makes a "report" thereto in writing. The identification of these reports and their location in public document collections are described at length in section C below.

Congressional Record. This is the official record of the proceedings, including debates, of each house of Congress. It is published daily while Congress is in session. A set of numbered and bound volumes, the "permanent" edition, is published for each session after its close. It should be noted that the permanent edition of the Congressional Record may not exactly reproduce the daily edition and that neither constitutes "a complete and verbatim account of the words spoken in the two houses."[93] Important for citation purposes is the fact that the paging differs in the two editions.

Since 1947 the last pages of each daily issue of the Congressional Record consist of a Daily Digest summarizing major activities in each chamber and noting, with page references to the proceedings, the introduction, reporting, passage, and approval or veto of bills. It also reports committee action not otherwise covered in the Congressional Record, notably with respect to hearings. In the permanent

93. See Schmeckbier and Eastin, supra note 92, at 139-142; Wasby, Legislative Materials as an Aid to Statutory Construction: A Caveat, 12 J. Pub. L. 262, 263-264 (1963); Cashman, Availability of Records of Legislative Debates, 24 Record of N.Y.C.B.A. 153-154 (1969).

edition, the Daily Digest pages from the daily issues are republished together as a separate part with the addition of a statistical résumé, a subject index, a table giving the public law numbers for bills enacted into public law, and the "History of Bills Enacted into Public Law" described in Section B below.

The permanent edition of the Congressional Record for each session also contains an index volume containing an "Index to the Proceedings" and another index entitled "History of Bills and Resolutions." The "Index to the Proceedings," hereinafter referred to as the general index, is an index by subject and name. Bills are listed under the appropriate subject headings by bill number only; page references for their history must be obtained by reference to the "History of Bills and Resolutions" as explained in section D below.

Publication of the Congressional Record began in December, 1873. Proceedings of Congress prior thereto were published for the periods indicated (but not always contemporaneously) in the following predecessor series: Annals of Congress (1789-1824), Register of Debates (1824-1837), and Congressional Globe (1833-1873).

Daily Digest. See Congressional Record above.

Digest of Public General Bills and Resolutions. This has been published for all sessions beginning in 1936 by the Library of Congress (formerly by its Legislative

Reference Service, presently by its Congressional Research Service). Five or more cumulative issues are published during each session of Congress, with biweekly supplementation as needed and a final edition at the close of the session. This publication, indexed by subject, summarizes each bill covered, indicates the committee reference, and states the last action taken. It also contains parallel reference tables for identical bills. Since 1967, it includes in addition brief legislative histories of each measure acted upon by either house, whether or not enacted into law.

Hearings. These contain oral views and written materials presented to committees of Congress in public proceedings. Their discovery and location are discussed in Section E below.

Journals. Both the Senate and the House publish journals of their proceedings, a separate volume for each chamber for each session of Congress. The House Journal and the Senate Journal together contain the same material that appears in the proceedings as published in the Congressional Record, except that neither journal includes debates or explanations and the Senate Journal does not include proceedings in executive session. Each volume contains a general index and a "History of Bills and Resolutions." Neither such "History," however, lists all action in the other body.

For some research purposes the two Journals may be used in lieu of the Congressional Record. They are not, however, as widely available as the latter. As to any particular bill it is necessary to consult both the Senate Journal and the House Journal; and the legislative history thus obtained does not include the debates. For these reasons this manual does not suggest use of the Journals as sources of legislative history except where the Congressional Record is not available.

The Senate proceedings (not including debates) in executive session are published in a separate Executive Journal, customarily some years after the period covered. If the executive session is open, however, the proceedings, including debates, are currently published in the Congressional Record. The use in legislative history research of Senate proceedings in executive session is confined to the function of that body with respect to the ratification of treaties, discussed in Part VII of this manual.

Monthly Catalog. The Monthly Catalog of United States Government Publications, issued by the Superintendent of Documents, Government Printing Office, is the only publication attempting to list as published all official federal publications. Although some publications not printed at the Government Printing Office (primarily processed items) are not included, for the purposes of this manual the Monthly Catalog may be considered as a complete listing.

While it lists other materials issued by Congress and its committees or otherwise relating to the legislative process, its primary use in legislative history research is to identify and locate Congressional committee hearings and, occasionally, reports or other documents of non-Congressional agencies relevant to but not reproduced in the Congressional source materials.

Slip law. A new law (once passed and either approved by the President, passed again over his veto, or having become a law upon his failure to return it within the constitutionally prescribed period) is first published separately on a single sheet of paper or more if necessary. Thus longer laws first appear as unbound pamphlets. The slip law is the first official publication of a statute and is then superseded by publication in the Statutes at Large, which are next described.

Statutes at Large. The United States Statutes at Large is the official compilation of the full (i.e., "at large") text of federal laws, concurrent resolutions, reorganization plans, proclamations, and constitutional amendments, Congress by Congress. (Treaties were formerly included but are now published in a separate series of books, for which see Part VII of this manual.) A numbered volume of these Statutes at Large is issued for each session of Congress. In them the public laws appear seriatim in chronological order. The same is true of private laws, but they are grouped separately and may or may not be placed in a separately bound "Part" of the numbered volume for that session.

United States Code. This is an official collection of currently operative statutory provisions of a general nature, topically arranged. It also contains the text of the Constitution and certain rules of court. Commercial publishers use the same material, similarly ordered, but add, following the statutory text of each section, "annotations" consisting of brief digests of pertinent cases and sometimes other materials. Both the official and commercial publications contain useful references to sources in the Statutes at Large, revisors' notes, related laws, etc. Cumulative supplements to the official Code are published annually, and the entire Code is revised at six-year intervals.

Weekly Compilation of Presidential Documents. This, published since 1965 by the Office of the Federal Register, contains listings of acts approved and texts or listings of Presidential messages, press releases accompanying approvals, and other materials released by the White House.

B. The Numbering System and Skeleton History

Since a legislative history is directed to some specific piece of legislation, the latter must first be identified by its designation in the official documents.

At the same time, particularly for more recent laws, it may be possible to construct a skeleton Congressional history of the item. These two things--the identification of a law and its vital statistics--are related in the doing. But it may be well for a beginner to have them in mind separately.

The numbering system. To begin a legislative history search it is first necessary to identify the bill by the bill number given it when it was introduced, the public law number given it when enacted, and the number (and session) of the Congress from which it emerged as a law. This three-point identification system must be known in order to use the necessary compilations, indexes, and other publications hereinafter mentioned. These numbers, except for the session number, appear on the slip law. All of them appear with the text of the statute as published later in the Statutes at Large. (But bill numbers were not carried in the Statutes at Large prior to volume 33 (1903) so that numbers for statutes enacted prior thereto should be obtained by consulting the general index to the Congressional Record or predecessor series for the appropriate session.) For public laws beginning in 1947, the bill number is also obtainable, if the public law number is known, from the bound volume of the Daily Digest. The bill number may also be located in various other sources including the Senate and House Journals, the U.S. Code Congressional and Administrative News published by West Publishing Company, the Congressional Index service of Commerce Clearing House, the Digest of Public General Bills and Resolutions, the entry for the slip law in the Government Printing Office Monthly Catalog, and the final edition of the House Calendar for the Congress which enacted it.

The public laws enacted during each Congress are serially numbered in chronological order of enactment. Private laws are similarly numbered in a separate series. Since 1957 the number of the Congress forms the first part of the public law number, e.g. Public Law 90-187, which means the 187th public law resulting from the 90th Congress but is read as one number. For measures enacted before 1957 a different form was used, e.g., Public Law 128, 84th Cong., 1st Sess. The public law number appears in all source notes in the United States Code for provisions enacted in 1957 or later; references therein to earlier provisions give the chapter number but not the public law number.[94] (Public Law is abbreviated Pub. L. in Code references; the preferred "White Book" citation is Pub. L. No.)

The session number, if not already obtained from the Statutes at Large or elsewhere, may quickly be ascer-

---

94. All federal statutes were formerly given chapter numbers in order as enacted, without differentiation as between public and private laws, beginning with ch. 1 in each session. The separate numbering of public and private laws, described in the text, was inaugurated shortly after the turn of the twentieth century. The chapter number, although important for citation purposes, has no particular significance in legislative history research. The use of chapter numbers was discontinued after 1956.

tained by reference to the Congressional Record since each volume of that series is identified by Congress and session as well as by volume number and date. But of course it is not necessary to look further than necessary, in any of these sources, to obtain the three numbers -- the bill number, the Congress (and session) number, and the public law number. Thereupon, with the use of these numbers, the research process is simply one of finding first the relevant documents and then the relevant statements or passages in them as explained below.

The skeleton history. With that necessary identification in mind, the next step for the researcher is to begin to develop the general procedural path of the legislation in its course of enactment (or, occasionally, its rejection). This skeleton history of a bill in Congress discloses the existence and location of committee reports, debates, hearings, and so on. Several tentative shortcuts for this purpose are possible if the law involved was enacted in recent years.

For statutes enacted in 1963 or later, a skeleton history is available in the Statutes at Large. Beginning with volume 77 (1963), each volume of public laws contains a "Guide to Legislative History of Bills Enacted into Public Law." This table lists the laws in order by public law number, and indicates for each the bill number and number of any companion bill, report numbers and committees reporting, the dates of consideration and passage by each house, and the Congressional Record volume (but not page) number. Similar information now also appears on each slip law as published, and since 1967 comparable but more detailed data appear in the Digest of Public General Bills and Resolutions.

For statutes enacted in 1947 or later, information of a similar nature may be obtained by consulting -- in the bound volume of the Daily Digest for the session in which the statute became law -- the table entitled "History of Bills Enacted into Public Law." This table lists all such bills in order by public law number together with the bill number, date of introduction, number of any companion bill originating in the other house, committees to which referred, dates and numbers of committee reports, date of passage by each house with a citation to the appropriate Congressional Record page indicating passage, and date of approval. Unfortunately, it does not furnish page references for other action or for debates and hence cannot be used in lieu of the index to the Congressional Record. But the skeleton legislative history thus provided in the Daily Digest is helpful as a basis for further research. For the years 1947 to 1961, inclusive, this table also indicated for each public law whether hearings were printed -- information not included in the indexes to the Congressional Record or in any of the published skeleton histories described above.

For the skeleton history of public laws enacted prior to 1947 (or private laws of any period), it is necessary to consult the appropriate index volume of the Congressional Record, following the procedures explained below in section D of this Part. (A skeleton history may also be obtained by consulting the indexes of both the Senate Journal and the House Journal for the session or sessions involved, but this is not recommended if the index volume of the Congressional Record is available.) Since it will be necessary in any event to locate the debates in the Congressional Record, the researcher may prefer to omit the shortcuts described above and turn directly to the appropriate index volume of that compilation for the skeleton history, even for recent statutes, as soon as he has obtained the necessary identification numbers.

C. Committee and Conference Reports

The next step, and the first in the matter of substance of the search, is to find and examine the committee reports in both houses as well as any conference report. They are the chief source of legislative history outside the Congressional Record. The reports are separately printed and numbered publications of the Senate or of the House of Representatives. They introduce an important additional numbering system. In both Senate and House the committee reports in each Congress are numbered serially and cited by number. For example, a Senate committee report will be cited "S. Rep. No." and a House committee report "H.R. Rep. No." followed, in either case, by the digits of the number and, for reports prior to 1969, by the number and session of the Congress[95] and the date. Beginning in 1969 the number of the Congress forms a part of the report number, *e.g.*, S. Rep. No. 91-128 (1969).

With occasional exceptions, the House and Senate reports are later reproduced in bound volumes comprising a separate series of the collection known as the "serial set" or "Congressional set." For each series in that collection there exists yet another numbering system, under which each volume is identified by what is known as the "serial number." For present purposes, however, it is unnecessary to describe the classification and numbering of the bound form of the reports, since they are cited in the same way as the separately printed reports and may be located in library collections by reference to that citation.

Except for conference reports, committee reports are not ordinarily published in the *Congressional Record*. (But conference reports are published in the *Senate* and *House Journals* as well as in the *Congressional Record*.)

---

95. Prior to 1881 there were some periods during which a new series of numbers for the reports of one or both houses of Congress began with each session. Although since that time the session number is technically unnecessary to identify a report, it aids in locating reports and its use in citation has been customary.

Recent reports may usually be obtained from the committee and from the House or Senate document room. For the official text of older reports persons outside the immediate area of Washington, D. C., will usually find it necessary to consult a library which has been designated as a depository library for government publications, of which there are several in every state. Not every committee report, however, is available in every such library. For example, from 1905 to 1938 reports on simple and concurrent resolutions (as well as those on private bills) were not distributed to depository libraries, although important public measures may result from investigations reported pursuant to such resolutions.[96] However, at least one report on the principal public bills enacted into law has for some years been reproduced by West Publishing Company in the series presently entitled U.S. Code Congressional and Administrative News. The Library of Congress will lend to any qualified library those Congressional reports and hearings published, roughly, since the beginning of the present century.[97]

For the period from 1789 until 1823 to 1838 (depending on the subject) the most important Congressional as well as Executive reports have been collected in the series

---

96. See Schmeckbier and Eastin, supra note 92, at 124, 128.

97. Elizabeth Finley, Crystal Gazing: The Problem of Legislative History, 45 A.B.A.J. 1281 (1959).

generally known as American State Papers.[98] These consist of one or more volumes containing materials on each of ten classes: Foreign Relations, Indian Affairs, Finance, Commerce and Navigation, Military Affairs, Naval Affairs, Post Office Department, Public Lands, Claims, and Miscellaneous.

D. Proceedings and Debates in Each House

Next in importance, and often even more important where changes are made by either house itself during the course of its consideration of committee recommendations, are the proceedings and debates of both houses. The relevant portions of these are to be found in the Congressional Record (or, for statutes enacted prior to December 1873, the appropriate predecessor series). There the first step is to consult the index volume for the session involved. Since a bill introduced in the first session may not receive final action until a later session, it is frequently necessary to consult the index volume for each session (normally two but sometimes more) of the Congress in which a law was enacted. (And of course if the history extends beyond a single Congress, bill and report numbers must be found for each as previously explained.) There, in the index entitled "History of Bills and Resolutions," see the entries under the number of the House or Senate bill or joint resolution in question. These in-

---

98. American State Papers, Documents, Legislative and Executive, of the Congress of the United States, published by Gales and Seaton in 38 volumes, 1832-1861.

dexes contain page references to the permanent edition of the Congressional Record for both the debates and action taken by either body on the particular measure during that session. They contain more detail than the skeleton histories described above. Unless there are complications such as some of those noted below, they provide for each enactment an outline of its complete history in Congress except for reference to hearings. (These indexes also furnish or confirm the report numbers of committee reports as well as the public or private law number for those bills and resolutions enacted into law.) In some of the earlier years the indexes are rather sketchy so that it may be necessary also to scan the text of the Congressional Record for the pertinent period.

With the page references at hand, it is a simple, if sometimestedious, matter to trace the history of the bill as it appears in the Congressional Record. Thus it may be found that a bill was introduced in the House without comment (as is ordinarily the case) in February, reported without amendment in March, and brought up for debate in April; that the chairman of the House committee read the full text of the committee report into the Congressional Record and stated on the floor that the purpose of the bill was as indicated in the first paragraph of that report; that the House forthwith passed the bill without discussion or amendment; that the bill was in the usual course transmitted to the Senate and referred to a committee, which reported it favorably in May; that later in that month the bill was brought up for action in the Senate, at which time the chairman of the Senate committee stated neither body had held hearings on the bill and then read into the Congressional Record the report of his committee, which merely endorsed the House report without qualification; that the Senate thereupon passed the bill without discussion or amendment; and that the President signed the bill a few days later. For such a statute, references to the action described above, with the text of the pertinent portions of the two committee reports and the remarks of the House committee chairman, will constitute the legislative history.

Most federal legislative histories, however, require more extensive search. It is usually necessary to locate and examine documents not reproduced in the Congressional Record, notably the committee reports (describedabove), and any hearings (described below). There are also special problems arising from such things as amendments, substitutions, continuations, multiple bills, post-veto measures, post-decisional bills, and appropriation acts. The following are some of the types of situations in which research in legislative history is more complicated:

Amendments. The bill may be reported with amendments by either or both committees, which usually are, but may not be, adopted; and amendments may be proposed on the floor of either or both houses, which may or may not be adopted. In such cases the text of the bill as introduced, the texts of all amendments proposed, and reasons given for their adoption or rejection, may be critical.[99]

Substitutions. Examination of the index may reveal that a House bill was substituted at some point for a Senate bill on the same subject. In this event, it will be necessary to search the complete history of both the House and the Senate bills.

Continuations. Examination of the reports or debates may reveal that the bill in question was the same as, or a modification of, a bill which had been introduced in a former Congress, on which hearings were held, but which failed of enactment. In such a case it will be necessary to trace the history of both the prior and the later proposals, noting any statements as to the purpose of the original proposal and of any changes made at the various stages of both proposals.

Multiple bills. Where reports or debates on a measure indicate it was one of a number of bills on the same general subject considered during the same period, the enactment of one in preference to another may be signifi-

---

99. The text of amendments adopted or proposed appears not only in the Congressional Record but also in the appropriate Senate or House Journal; the latter, however, contain no comment or debate.

cant.[100] In this situation, it may be necessary to consult the general index to the Congressional Record for each session of one or more Congresses and trace the history of the several bills, examining comparable provisions in each with care to note any reasons stated for selection of the provision finally enacted. As a preliminary to this type of search, it may be helpful to consult the Digest of Public General Bills and Resolutions for the appropriate period.

Post-veto measures. A bill may be reported with the statement that it was designed to avoid an objection voiced by the President in vetoing a similar bill -- in which case the veto message (published in the Congressional Record, in the journal of the originating house, and usually also as a separate House or Senate document) as well as the legislative history of the prior bill will be pertinent. The Congressional Record and Daily Digest indexes show when a bill has been vetoed and returned to Congress with a veto message, whether before adjournment or, as has sometimes happened, after adjournment. For "pocket vetoes" (i.e., after adjournment) as to which no message is issued, however, the only regular listing is in the final issue of the House Calendar for each Congress. Notations of pocket vetoes are, however, included in the skeleton histories published in the Digest of Public

100. See, e.g., Hannah v. Larche, 363 U.S. 420, 434-39 (1960), in which construction of the Civil Rights Act of 1957 was based principally on deliberate legislative selection of one bill rather than another under consideration at the same time which varied in important details.

General Bills and Resolutions. Occasional notation of a pocket veto appears in the Weekly Compilation of Presidential Documents. For all measures vetoed prior to 1969, a useful listing has been compiled by the Senate Library.[101]

Post-decisional bills. Some measures are designed to change the effect of a decision of the Supreme Court or other court interpreting an act of Congress. In that event the court's holding, and perhaps the legislative history of the statute prior thereto, may be pertinent.

Appropriation acts. Occasionally it is necessary to leaf through hundreds of pages of intermittent debates on a lengthy appropriation measure in order to discover a passage relating to one brief provision of general law enacted as a rider to the appropriation bill.

E. Committee Hearings and Related Bills

On most bills of importance hearings are held by committees of one or both houses of Congress. A check of the committee reports on the bill will usually reveal if hearings were held. The fact is also frequently mentioned in the debates. The research problems involved, apart from discovering

---

101. Presidential Vetoes: Record of Bills Vetoed and Action Taken Thereon by the Senate and House of Representatives, First Congress through the Ninetieth Congress, 1789-1968, compiled by the Senate Library, printed for the use of the office of the Secretary of the Senate (Gov't Printing Office, 1969). This publication lists by President, Congress, and session formal vetoes and pocket vetoes with references to the Congressional Record or its predecessors for subsequent action.

whether or not hearings were held or published, are mainly those of procuring copies or access to them and to the text of the bills to which they relate. The relatively minor role which hearings play in legislative histories has been previously mentioned. Hearings are only occasionally of importance on specific issues. But sometimes they contain valuable background information. They may be essential where the subject is a general one for scholarly purposes. Where counsel are engaged in a day-to-day representation of private or governmental interests which require to be kept informed of every development, proposal, or consideration as it occurs, hearings are the active arena in which they participate or which they report -- a function beyond the subject of this manual. For present purposes, hearings supply supplemental information for interpretative problems after, sometimes long after, the legislative process has been concluded.

It should be noted also that many Congressional hearings do not relate to specific bills but are in the nature of more or less broad investigation of problems respecting particular subjects. Important legislation may result from these hearings, in which event the hearings may furnish valuable background material. References to any such prior history will ordinarily appear in the reports and other legislative materials relating to the resulting bills.

Published hearings. Hearings are usually published, although not invariably. For current legislative proposals, the Congressional Index, a looseleaf service published by Commerce Clearing House, indicates for each bill whether hearings have been printed. From 1947 through 1961 this information also appeared in the bound volume of the Daily Digest for each session of Congress.

When published, hearings are issued as separate publications, customarily in paperback form, of the Senate or House committee involved. (Lengthy or interrupted hearings may be published in several numbered pamphlets, designated "Parts.") They do not comprise any regular series of Congressional publications and hence, unlike bills and reports, cannot be identified by a numbering system.[102] The titles of published hearings ordinarily indicate the numbers of the bills under consideration. In many instances, however, that information is contained in a subtitle and the main title refers only to the subject of the proposed legislation, or to its short title or popular name or that of a prior act it is designed to amend. To facilitate identification and location of hearings, a careful note should be made of any references to them discovered in the reports or debates, including the full title and exact dates if given.

---

102. Serial numbering systems for their hearings have been inaugurated in recent years by a few committees, *e.g.*, the House Committee on Interstate and Foreign Commerce.

At this point in the search -- whether or not he has a complete citation for the hearings -- the researcher should be in possession of the name of the committee in each house to which the bill in question was referred and the number and session of the Congress during which any hearings on that bill would have been held. For most proposals he can also pinpoint possible hearing dates in the respective houses to two periods -- one between the date of introduction of the bill and the date of the report of the committee in the originating house, and the other between approval of the first house and the date of the report of the committee in the other house. With this information at hand, published hearings may be identified (and their existence verified) by recourse to one or more of several listings.

Hearings are listed in the current issues of the Monthly Catalog where they may be located under the name of the committee as well as by subject. There are also earlier general catalogs of government publications listing hearings prior to 1941.[103] Various checklists of published Congressional hearings have also been issued from time to time. For the period up to March 1923, the most complete of these is the Checklist of Hearings before Congressional Committees through the 67th Congress, published by the Reference Depart-

---

103. The biennial Document Catalog, covering the period 1894-1940, and Checklist of United States Public Documents, 1789-1909 (3d. ed., 1911), both issued by the Superintendent of Documents, Gov't Printing Office.

ment of the Library of Congress in nine parts, 1957-1959, which listing covers all hearings of which record has been found and indicates the source or location for items not in that Library. Several indexes have been published of hearings to be found in the Senate and House libraries, which, however, do not include all hearings published, particularly those in the early years.[104] It is also possible to verify the existence (but not the publication) of hearings, and to obtain their dates, by reference to the subject index in the bound volume of the Daily Digest for the session or sessions involved; this procedure is, however, more involved and less productive than reference to the listings noted above.

While the supply lasts, printed hearings are usually obtainable from the committee before which they have been held. Occasionally they are sold by the Superintendent of Documents. Older hearings are difficult to obtain, particularly since it was not until 1938 that Congress provided for distribution of committee publications to depository

---

104. U.S. Congress. Senate Library. Index of Congressional Committee Hearings ... prior to January 3, 1935, in the U.S. Senate Library (Govt. Printing Office 1935).

Same. Cumulative Index of Congressional Committee Hearings ... from 74th Congress (Jan. 3, 1935) through 85th Congress (Jan. 3, 1959) in the U.S. Senate Library (Govt. Printing Office 1959). Quadrennial Supplement, Jan. 7, 1959 to Jan. 3, 1963 (1963). Second Quadrennial Supplement, 1963 through Jan. 3, 1967 (1967).

U.S. Congress. House Library. Index of Congressional Committee Hearings in the Library of the U.S. House of Representatives prior to January 1, 1951. (Govt. Printing Office 1954). Supplement, 1949-January 1955 (1956).

libraries. But, as indicated above, those published during the twentieth century may be made available through inter-library loan from the Library of Congress.

When the existence and publication of hearings have been ascertained and copies have been procured, the search for usable parts may entail considerable care and ingenuity. While some hearings are indexed, many are not. Frequently they must be leafed through in an effort to single out statements which may be relied on to establish either the condition Congress sought to remedy by a particular provision or the effect the bill's original proponents -- or opponents -- believed that it would have on existing law.

Texts of bills. If a bill has been amended before enactment, it is of course vital to obtain the text of the original bill and the text of the amendments, or the text of the amended bill at each stage. Frequently it may be important to have the text of amendments proposed but not adopted. For recent bills, the prints (as introduced, as reported, as received in the second body, as reported in the second body, and very frequently unofficial committee prints at various stages) are usually obtainable from individual Congressmen or from the appropriate committee. Separate prints of older bills are virtually impossible to obtain. The bill as introduced is always printed in the hearings, if any, but ordinarily the committee reports print only those portions specifically amending existing law. The complete text of the bill may or may not be printed at any one place in the Congressional Record, although major bills are usually printed as read and discussed section by section when brought up for vote in each body. Ordinarily, however, with the hearings and reports at hand, a close reading of the debates, including the text of amendments adopted, will make it possible to reconstruct the text of the bill as it existed at any particular stage.

F. Reproductions, Collections, Current Measures

The scarcity of older federal legislative history materials has been considerably alleviated in recent years through issuance, by both federal and commercial agencies, of microfacsimile editions and compilations. Materials so reproduced include the Congressional Record and its predecessors; hearings 1869-1934; and compilations of the legislative history materials for selected major statutes since 1951. These materials are available only in libraries subscribing to major groups or series of such reproductions.

Particularly valuable are compilations in book form of all or major portions of the legislative history materials relating to particular federal statutes. A number have been published, some by government offices and some by private publishers. Among the statutes so covered are the

Food, Drug, and Cosmetic Act of 1938 and the Wheeler-Lea Act of 1938,[105] the Administrative Procedure Act of 1946,[106] the Labor-Management Relations Act of 1947,[107] the Atomic Energy Act of 1954,[108] the Labor-Management Reporting and Disclosure Act of 1959,[109] the Occupational Safety and Health Act of 1970,[110] and various revenue acts.[111] There are also some guides to the legislative history of particular statutes,

---

105. Charles W. Dunn, Federal Food, Drug, and Cosmetic Act: A Statement of Its Legislative Record (New York, G. E. Stechert & Co., 1938) traces the legislative history of the various proposals beginning in 1933, as well as of the act finally enacted in 1938, reproducing the text of the pertinent reports and debates and the hearings presentations of government spokesmen. Charles W. Dunn, Wheeler-Lea Act: A Statement of Its Legislative Record (New York, G. E. Stechert & Co., 1938), has a similar format.

106. Senate Committee on the Judiciary, Administrative Procedure Act: Legislative History, S. Doc. No. 248, 79th Cong., 2d. Sess. (1946).

107. National Labor Relations Board, Legislative History of the Labor-Management Relations Act, 1947 (2 v., Gov't Printing Office, 1948).

108. Atomic Energy Commission, Legislative History of the Atomic Energy Act of 1954, Public Law 703, 83d Congress (3 v., Gov't Printing Office, 1955).

109. National Labor Relations Board, Legislative History of the Labor-Management Reporting and Disclosure Act of 1959 (2 v., Gov't Printing Office, 1959). Much of the same material, arranged by titles and keyed by subject, appears in Department of Labor, Legislative History of the Labor-Management Reporting and Disclosure Act of 1959, Titles I-VI (Gov't Printing Office, 1964).

110. Bureau of National Affairs, The Job Safety and Health Act of 1970; Text, Analysis, Legislative History (Washington, 1971), reproducing the full text of the reports and significant portions of the debates.

111. See Part V below.

giving references to pertinent documents[112] as well as some early lists and compilations covering statutes respecting particular subjects such as agriculture, copyright, tariffs, and trusts.[113] In addition, the increasing use of legislative histories has spurred the collection by some libraries of materials relating to particular federal statutes.[114]

If the statute under investigation was enacted during the current session, or a session so recent that the bound Congressional Record is not yet available, the procedures will be somewhat different. Ordinarily, as noted above, the various prints of the bill or resolution, as well as the hearings and reports, will be readily available. Action taken can be traced through the biweekly indexes to the Congressional Record and through its Daily Digest as well as the House Calendar, and through the cumulative issues of

---

112. An older but still very useful work of this nature is Clarence A. Miller, The Legislative Evolution of the Interstate Commerce Act (Washington, John Byrne & Co., 1930), which contains a guide to the legislative history of the 1887 act and of each amendment to 1930.

113. For a listing and description of these earlier materials on special subjects, see Schmeckbier, supra note 92, at 148-150.

114. The Union List of Legislative Histories: 47th Congress, 1883 - 89th Congress, 1966, issued by the Law Librarians' Society of Washington, D. C. (Vienna, Va., Coiner Publications, 1967), lists federal statutes for which various libraries in the Washington area have compiled legislative history materials, including hearings, reports, debates, and frequently other materials such as executive communications or special studies. As to each library, it is indicated whether outsiders are permitted access; in most instances the materials may not be withdrawn, but some of the libraries permit borrowing by another library.

the Digest of Public General Bills and Resolutions. The debates can be followed in the daily issues of the Congressional Record. Hearings scheduled and in progress are noted in the Daily Digest.

Several private reporting services may also be used to ascertain the status of pending public measures, identify the relevant materials, and trace the legislative history of recently enacted public laws. A useful work is the Congressional Index, published by Commerce Clearing House. A new edition, in looseleaf form, is issued for each Congress and is brought up to date by semiweekly reports while Congress is in session. A bill or resolution may be located by bill number, subject, short title, or sponsor. If it has become law, it may also be located by public law number. Status tables indicate for each bill or resolution the date of introduction and committee reference; dates of hearings and availability thereof; date and number of each committee report with or without amendments; dates of floor amendments and passage by each house; and date of approval. Numbers of companion and identical bills are also supplied. Hearings not directed to particular bills may also be located by committee.

Beginning in 1970 Congressional Information Service has issued an annual and a monthly publication, entitled respectively CIS/Annual and CIS/Index. Both publications furnish brief abstracts of all hearings, reports, committee prints, and other Congressional documents issued during the period covered. These abstracts may be located by bill or resolution number, report or document number, subject, name, title, or committee. In addition, the annual volumes contain for each public law (in order by public law number) an outline of its legislative history with references to all related hearings and other Congressional documents.

The U.S. Code Congressional and Administrative News, published by the West Publishing Company, is issued in semimonthly pamphlets while Congress is in session and monthly at other times. Bound volumes are published at the end of each session, superseding the pamphlets. This publication reproduces the full text of at least one report on the principal public laws. All issues also contain cumulative tables giving for each public law an outline of its legislative history similar to that provided on the slip laws and in the Statutes at Large.

Congressional Quarterly, Inc., publishes an annual Congressional Quarterly Almanac, covering the preceding session of Congress, and the Congressional Quarterly Weekly Reports. Each covers major Congressional action whether or not it has resulted in legislation. Materials are arranged and located by subject matter. There is also a table listing enacted public laws with a brief legislative history of each. These publications state in considerable detail, frequently with extensive excerpts, the contents of hearings, reports, debates, and other sources respecting the various measures covered.

There are a great number of commercial reporting services devoted to particular fields of public law, e.g., labor law, trade regulation, public utilities, food and drugs. Among the principal publishers are the Bureau of National Affairs, Commerce Clearing House, Matthew Bender, Pike and Fischer, and Prentice-Hall. All such services issue periodic or special reports noting current Congressional developments in the field covered. They frequently furnish considerable detail respecting pending or recently enacted measures, in some instances reproducing excerpts from or the full text of bills and pertinent reports and other basic source materials. Some of the materials so made available respecting federal taxation are noted below in Part V of this manual.

Much of the current legislative history material made available by the commercial services would be of considerable utility to the researcher in later years, when official prints or unofficial commentary may not be easily obtained. But the services supply such materials primarily in the form of pamphlets or leaflets (or eventually replaced looseleaf pages) which seldom remain indefinitely in a library collection. When these become unavailable, the search

for legislative history from official or other standard sources -- as described above -- must again be utilized.

PART V

ADDITIONAL SOURCES FOR TAX LAWS

The basic materials of legislative history of tax statutes, and the principles governing their use, are the same as for other federal statutes. However, the extreme complexity of modern tax laws, their kaleidoscopic amendment, and the constitutional requirement that they originate in the House of Representatives[115] have led to the development of a rather specialized process for their enactment. It involves the intensive participation of a greater variety of Congressional and executive bodies and the production of an imposing and detailed body of materials designed to influence or explain Congressional action. All these result in some shifts in relative emphasis on particular elements of legislative history. It is also a field in which commercial publishers have been active, which underscores the importance of legislative history in the interpretation of statutes generally. Detailed descriptions of the process of enactment of federal tax legislation have been published.[116]

---

115. Art. I, § 7.

116. See Stanley S. Surrey and William C. Warren, Federal Income Taxation: Cases and Materials, 36-40 (Brooklyn, Foundation Press, 1962); Roy Blough, The Federal Taxing Process, 66-88 (New York, Prentice-Hall, 1952); Laurence N. Woodworth, Procedures Followed by Congress in Enacting Tax Legislation and the Role of the Joint Committee Staff in that Process, U. So. Cal. 1966 Tax Inst. 21; John F. Manley, The Politics of Finance: The House Committee on Ways and Means (Little, Brown, 1970); Surrey, Congress and the Tax Lobbyist -- How Special Tax Provisions Get Enacted, 70 Harv. L. Rev. 1145 (1957).

Only the principal respects in which this process differs from that applicable to other federal bills are noted here.

Although the typical non-tax bill is introduced prior to hearing (and tax bills may be so introduced), major tax proposals today are customarily considered in hearings before the House Committee on Ways and Means prior to introduction of a bill. These proposals usually originate in recommendationsmade to Congress by the President or Secretary of the Treasury. Also -- as is true of other bills -- the genesis of a tax measure is sometimes traceable to earlier studies or investigations. The Tax Reform Act of 1969, for example, had its inception in studies made by the Treasury Department over a five-year period preceding the House committee hearings which resulted in the introduction of the bill.[117] Similarly, hearings and studies by the House Committee on Ways and Means, although not at the time resulting in enactment of legislation, may be important sources of later reform proposals.[118]

It is the practice of the House committee to publish the proposals in considerable detail in advance of the hearing. After the hearing the committee in executive

117. See Tax Reform Studies and Proposals, U.S. Treasury Department, Pts. 1-4, published jointly as a committee print by the House Committee on Ways and Means and the Senate Committee on Finance, 91st Cong., 1st Sess. (1969).

118. See, e.g., Tax Revision Compendium, a collection of papers respecting broadening of the tax base, submitted to the Ways and Means Committee in connection with panel discussions conducted by the committee beginning November 16, 1959, published in three volumes as a committee print, 86th Cong., 1st Sess. (1959).

session decides upon the substance of the provisions to be embodied in the measure -- which may or may not be in essential accord with the Administration proposals -- and finally agrees upon a draft bill incorporating its decisions. Although proceedings in executive session are not reported, the House committee from time to time issues press releases announcing its tentative or final decisions respecting particular subjects. A bill agreed upon is then introduced and referred pro forma to the same committee.[119] Shortly thereafter the committee submits its report recommending passage of the bill and explaining its provisions. This report, reflecting the determinations made in executive session, is a highly persuasive component of the legislative history.[120] It consists of a general explanation of the measure, followed by a technical explanation of its detail.

The bill is usually considered by the full House under a "closed rule" greatly restricting debate and limiting amendments to those offered by the committee. Hence floor amendments are virtually impossible although technically

---

119. This seemingly circuitous procedure is necessary because the rules of the House require that every bill be referred to a committee, and that every committee recommendation for the enactment of a bill be accompanied by a written report.

120. This is not to say, however, that the committee report is always accepted at face value. See, e.g., American Automobile Ass'n v. United States, 367 U.S. 687, 695 (1961), in which the Court rejected argument, based in part on a statement to that effect in a House report, that no change in the law had been effected where Congress enacted two new Code provisions and repealed them the following year.

they may be effected via a motion to recommit. The House debates should never be neglected by the seeker of legislative history, however, since tax bills must originate in that chamber and statements there, particularly those by committee spokesmen, are frequently of considerable importance.

After passage by the House, the bill is transmitted to the Senate, where it is referred to the Senate Committee on Finance. Hearings before that committee, since they begin with a specific bill rather than a generalized proposal, may sometimes contain more detailed explication of the language of particular provisions than do the House hearings. But the latter are, in general, at least as important as the Senate hearings as sources of legislative intent. In both House and Senate hearings, statements of the Treasury Department are of particular significance. Frequently they are the only source for important information on the problems to which the legislation is addressed. They may be useful not only in interpretation of enacted provisions but also as supporting arguments based on failure of Congress to enact Administration proposals.[121]

The Senate committee sometimes proposes major changes in the House-approved bill. In such instances, of course, explanatory data in the Senate report and debates will be especially important. The Senate report, unlike

121. See, *e.g.*, Fribourg Navigation Co. v. Commissioner, 383 U.S. 272, 284-85 (1966).

that of the House committee, may incorporate both general or policy explanation and technical explanation in a single format. Floor amendments are more common in the Senate. The debates may also be considerably longer than in the House. As is true of other legislation, where differences between the versions of the bill approved by the two houses are resolved in conference, the conference report and accompanying statement, as well as the remarks by the House and Senate conferees in the subsequent debates, are vital sources of legislative history with respect to the provisions involved.

The ranking members of the Ways and Means (House) and Finance (Senate) Committees comprise the Joint Committee on Internal Revenue Taxation. Although that committee is not directly concerned with the enactment of legislation, its staff serves as technical tax staff for both the Ways and Means Committee and the Finance Committee. The staff participates with the Treasury Department in drafting the original tax proposal, advises the House and Senate Legislative Counsel (as does also the Tax Legislative Counsel of the Treasury Department) in the drafting of tax bills and amendments, and prepares supplemental materials for the use of the committees. The Joint Committee staff also prepares the general explanation contained in the committee reports. The technical explanation originates with the Internal Revenue Service or the Tax Legislative Counsel of the Treasury Department, or both. The reports are further perfected in joint meetings of the Joint Committee staff, the Treasury staff (Tax Legislative Counsel), Internal Revenue Service (Legislation and Regulations Division of Chief Counsel), and the Legislative Counsel of the appropriate house of Congress.

The participation of the above-mentioned offices in the drafting of tax legislative materials is noteworthy, for purposes of this manual, because it brings to bear a degree of expertise not available for many subjects of proposed legislation. The use of a single technical staff to serve both a House and a Senate committee, in particular, is unique to the tax field. It should, however, be borne in mind that the legislative history materials may properly be used as reflecting only the intent of their formal authors. A committee report, for example, evinces the intent of the committee (and of the house to which it reports) even though many other persons may have aided in its drafting.

The procedure for locating these materials of tax legislative history varies from that applicable to other federal statutes only in that these materials have been made more readily available both through special collections and reprints and through rapid reporting services. Principal aids of this nature are described below.[122]

Invaluable for materials preceding the Internal Revenue Code of 1954 are the several volumes of the Seidman series of commercially published histories, as follows:

> Seidman's Legislative History of Federal Income and Excess Profits Tax Laws, 1953-1939 (2 v., New York, Prentice-Hall, 1954)
>
> Seidman's Legislative History of Federal Income Tax Laws, 1938-1861 (New York, Prentice-Hall, 1938)
>
> Seidman's Legislative History of Excess Profits Tax Laws, 1946-1917 (New York, Prentice-Hall, 1947)

In these compilations there may be found for each section or paragraph of the Internal Revenue Code of 1939 as amended to the date of publication, and of individual revenue acts preceding that Code, excerpts or digests of pertinent discussion in the Congressional reports, debates, and hearings as well as staff reports of the Joint Committee. Similar material is also included as to unenacted related provisions.

The Internal Revenue Service, in its Cumulative Bulletin 1939-1, pt. 2, reprinted seriatim the text of the House and Senate reports and conference reports if any, on

---

122. For a useful description of these and other materials of federal tax bibliography see Allen D. Altman, A Guide to Tax Research, 22 U. Miami L. Rev. 836 (1968).

all the revenue acts and acts amendatory thereof from 1913 through 1938, deleting some matter considered irrelevant or unnecessary. With respect to subsequent revenue acts (with the exception of the 1954 Code), the same materials are reprinted in the Cumulative Bulletin for the year in which the statute was enacted except that, where the Senate and House reports are substantially the same, only one is reproduced. Many, but not all, of these reports appear earlier in the weekly Internal Revenue Bulletin issued by the Internal Revenue Service.

For the Revenue Act of 1948, coverage similar to the Seidman compilations is provided by Paul Wolkin and Marcus Manoff, eds., Revenue Act of 1948 (Albany, Matthew Bender, 1948).

The full texts of the House, Senate, and conference reports on the Internal Revenue Code of 1954 as originally enacted were reprinted in various unofficial publications, of which one is still readily available, the permanent edition of U.S. Code Congressional and Administrative News, 1954, vol. 3. Statements of the respective committee chairmen summarizing the bill as introduced, as reported by the Senate committee, and as agreed to by the conference committee were reprinted from the Congressional Record by the same publisher, following the text of the enactment, in a volume entitled Internal Revenue Code of 1954 (1954).

For acts amending the 1954 Code, the West Publishing Company has made available continuations of the last-mentioned volume as follows: Internal Revenue Acts Beginning 1954 (1961), covering enactments 1954-1960; Internal Revenue Acts Beginning 1961 (1966), covering enactments 1961-1965; and Internal Revenue Acts 1966-1970 (1971). In these the text of the statutes is followed by the text of the principal reports on each with indication of the identifying number of each report not reproduced. Both the 1966 and 1971 volumes also reproduce some of the debates. In the latter may also be found the dates of consideration and passage in each house. In all of this series, materials not directly affecting the Internal Revenue Code are omitted. For each such act, also, at least one Congressional report has been reprinted in the U.S. Code Congressional and Administrative News for the year of enactment as well as in the Cumulative Bulletin, as noted above. (The Index volume of the looseleaf service, Standard Federal Tax Reporter, published by Commerce Clearing House, contains a checklist, arranged by Code sections, giving for each act amending the 1954 Code references to the Cumulative Bulletin reproducing the pertinent committee reports.)

With respect to particular sections of the 1954 Code as amended, a variety of unofficial publications provide ready reference to much, although not all, of the pertinent official legislative history materials. Of these, the most complete coverage is provided by Rabkin and Johnson, Federal Income, Gift and Estate Taxation, a looseleaf encyclopedia published by Matthew Bender. This publication presently has four volumes devoted to "Code and Congressional Reports," which furnish for each Code section excerpts from House, Senate, and conference reports on the 1954 Code as well as all amendatory acts. Also the United States Code Annotated furnishes for each section page references to the appropriate reports as reproduced in U.S. Code Congressional and Administrative News. The Federal Code Annotated contains numerous excerpts from committee reports. Excerpts or references to the reports appear following the appropriate Code sections in the looseleaf services published by Commerce Clearing House (Standard Federal Tax Reporter, Federal Excise Tax Reporter, and Federal Estate and Gift Tax Reporter) and Prentice-Hall (Federal Taxes). Similar materials, and occasional references to committee proposals not enacted, appear as annotations in the multi-volume looseleaf encyclopedia, Mertens, Law of Federal Income Taxation, published by Callaghan & Company (1942- , with current supplementation and periodic revision).

For some recent tax acts the House Committee on Ways and Means has published special compilations reproducing their complete legislative history except, in some cases, for the full text of hearings. Statutes so covered include, among others, the Revenue Acts of 1962 and 1964, the Interest

Equalization Tax Act of 1964, and the Tax Adjustment Act of 1966. For each statute the compilation includes a statement of the chronological history, the hearings (in full text, digests, or a combination), reports, debates, excerpts from presidential messages, committee press releases, the text of the bill at various stages, and a summary of the bill as enacted prepared by the staff of the Joint Committee.

Occasionally published, but not always made available to the public, are materials prepared by the Joint Committee staff for use of the committees such as summaries of hearing testimony, summaries of Senate amendments, and the like. The Senate Finance Committee sometimes publishes a technical memorandum of the position of the Treasury Department on a particular bill at the stage of consideration by that committee.

Microform reproductions of the basic legislative history materials have been issued for all of the revenue acts from 1909 to 1950 and a number of the later acts as well as for the Internal Revenue Codes of 1939 and 1954.

For very recent or pending legislation, ordinarily the most timely and complete coverage is afforded by the specialized commercial services. The <u>Standard Federal Tax Reporter</u> (Commerce Clearing House) has a "Pending Legislation" section covering major pending bills and other pertinent bills reported. The text of bills is reproduced and information is provided as to their status as well as the Code sections affected. Federal Taxes (Prentice-Hall) has a "New Legislation" section covering recent statutes and pending bills, containing similar material as well as excerpts from reports and occasionally committee or White House press releases. Subscriptions to these services also include weekly and special reports noting action taken or scheduled on pending legislation and for important proposals the text, excerpts, or summaries of bills, reports, hearings, debates, and other official documents as well as editorial explanations. Information and commentary on developments at various stages in the legislative process are also furnished with subscriptions to the Tax Coordinator (Research Institute of America), Rabkin and Johnson's Federal Income, Gift and Estate Taxation (Matthew Bender), and in the periodical U.S. Tax Week (Matthew Bender).

PART VI

SOURCES FOR CONSTITUTIONAL PROVISIONS

What may be called the legislative history of constitutional provisions differs greatly from that of statutes because such provisions emerge not alone from a legislative assembly through settled routines but from conventions or commissions, public debates, and legislatures when they submit or ratify amendments. Moreover, the source materials and adoption process differ with respect to (A) the formulation and adoption of the original Constitution of the United States, (B) the later Bill of Rights attached thereto, and (C) subsequent amendments. State constitutional history must also be differentiated in the first and third of these respects.

A. The Federal Constitution of 1789

There is an extensive secondary literature on the history of the adoption of the original United States Constitution.[123] It covers the general background of post-

123. No bibliography of the extensive body of secondary literature recounting the history of the adoption of the Constitution can be attempted here. Particularly valuable are the following: Charles Warren, The Making of the Constitution (first published 1928; rev. ed., Little, Brown, 1937); Andrew C. McLaughlin, The Confederation and the Constitution, 1783-1789 (first published 1905; reprinted, with introduction and bibliography, Crowell-Collier Pub. Co., 1962); Carl Van Doren, The Great Rehearsal (New York, Viking Press, 1948); and Clinton Rossiter, 1787: The Grand Convention (Macmillan Co., 1966); Max Farrand, The Framing of the Constitution of the United States (first published 1913; rev. ed., Yale U. Press, 1962); the introduction to Edward

Revolution problems as reflected in the proceedings of the Continental Congress culminating in the proposal of that body for a constitutional convention; the actual drafting of the Constitution in the Philadelphia convention of 1787; its consideration and submission to the states by the Congress; the efforts of its proponents to secure, and of its opponents to prevent, public acceptance; and its ratification by the state conventions from 1787 to 1790.[124]

The formal documents of the Continental Congress directly concerned with the Constitution -- e.g., the resolutions convening the Philadelphia convention and submitting the proposed Constitution -- are reproduced in several of the compilations noted below with respect to the Philadelphia convention. But occasionally it may be helpful to explore in more detail the activities of that Congress in order to trace the historical background of a proposal adopted or rejected in the Philadelphia convention or in the early years of the United States Congress, or to determine the then accepted meaning of a particular phrase in the Consti-

---

Dumbauld, The Constitution of the United States (U. of Okla. Press, 1964); and Francis Newton Thorpe, Constitutional History of the United States 1765-1895 (3 v., Callaghan & Co., 1901, reprinted by Da Capo Press 1970).

124. Two states ratified the Constitution after its effective date and after the Bill of Rights had been submitted to the states (North Carolina in November 1789, Rhode Island in 1790). Hence the proceedings in the ratifying conventions in those states are not actually legislative history materials of either the 1789 Constitution or the Bill of Rights. The earlier North Carolina convention of 1788, which refused to ratify, made proposals which may properly be considered as legislative history of the Bill of Rights.

tution or a statute.[125] For these purposes, the principal sources are the following: The Journals of the Continental Congress, covering the years from 1774 to 1789, of which several editions were published. Although the Journals contain the text of many reports and other communications, they do not contain the debates and are incomplete in other respects. The Library of Congress edition of the Journals, however, published by the Government Printing Office in 34 volumes (1904-37), included the record of portions of the proceedings originally withheld as secret. That edition also reprinted as appendixes most of the notes of the debates privately made by Jefferson, John Adams, and Madison. Madison's notes, covering the periods 1782-83 and February-April 1787, were also reprinted in the 1845 edition and later reprints of Elliot's Debates, mentioned below. The collected writings of each of those three include their respective debate notes. Edmund Cody Burnett, ed., Letters of the Members of the Continental Congress (8 v., Washington, Carnegie Inst., 1921-36), contains notes of the debates and proceedings made by other members of the Congress as well as both official and private correspondence and other documents, all in chronological order. Indispensable as a

---

125. For an example of the use of Madison's notes of the debates in the Continental Congress, as reproduced in Elliot's Debates, see Knowlton v. Moore, 178 U.S. 41, 96-101 (1900), wherein the Court referred to those proceedings at considerable length as supporting its construction of the uniformity requirement of Art. I, § 9 of the Constitution.

guide to the history and activities of the Congress is the single volume by the same editor-author, The Continental Congress (New York, Macmillan Co., 1941).

The Philadelphia convention itself met behind closed doors. Its debates were not officially recorded. Its rather inadequate journal was not published until 1819. The earliest generally available source of information as to the intent of the framers of the Constitution, therefore, consisted of unofficial statements made by them and their supporters in the public press or pamphlets during the campaign to secure the adoption of the Constitution. In the early years of the Republic, consequently, there arose a judicial practice of resorting to such public statements, as well as private records and correspondence, in construing provisions of the Constitution. The most noted of such statements were a series of 85 essays written by Hamilton, Madison, and Jay under the pseudonym "Publius." First printed in newspapers in 1787-1788, the papers were printed in book form as The Federalist, of which many editions have since been published.[126] Although there has been some con-

---

126. Among the numerous modern editions are one edited by Benjamin Fletcher Wright and published in 1961 by Belknap Press of Harvard University Press; a paperback edition with an introduction by Clinton Rossiter, published in 1961 by The New American Library of World Literature (Mentor); and a 1945 edition with an introduction by Carl Van Doren published by Heritage Press.

flict in scholarly opinion as to the influence of The Federalist on the ratification of the Constitution,[127] there is no question that it has always been accorded great weight in interpretation of the Constitution.[128]

Other essays and pamphlets of the period, both advocating and opposing ratification, many of which were written by members of the Philadelphia or state conventions, are readily available in two principal collections.[129]

Private records of the proceedings and debates of the Philadelphia convention were kept by a number of delegates. Beginning in 1821 with those of Robert Yates,[130] they have been discovered or released from time to time

---

127. See Gottfried Dietze, The Federalist: A Classic on Federalism and Free Government, 4 n.3 (Johns Hopkins Press, 1960).

128. See Dietze, supra, at 5-7. From the beginning, the Supreme Court made references to The Federalist in expounding the Constitution. E.g., Cohens v. Virginia, 19 U.S. (6 Wheat.) 264, 418-20 (1821). For criticism of reliance on Madison's writings in The Federalist see William W. Crosskey, Politics and the Constitution, I, 8-12 (U. of Chicago Press, 1953).

129. Paul Leicester Ford, ed., Essays on the Constitution of the United States, Published during its Discussion by the People 1787-1788 (Brooklyn, Historical Printing Club, 1892); and, by the same editor, Pamphlets on the Constitution of the United States (first published 1888; reprinted, Da Capo Press, 1968). A selection of the principal writings in opposition to ratification is contained in Morton Borden, ed., The Antifederalist Papers (Mich. State U. Press, 1965).

130. Secret Proceedings and Debates of the Convention at Philadelphia, in the Year 1787, for the Purpose of Forming the Constitution of the United States of America: From Notes taken by the late Robert Yates, Esq., Chief Justice of New York, and copied by John Lansing, Jun., Esq., late Chancellor of that State, Member of that Convention . . . (Albany, N. Y., 1821). Yates' notes do not cover the entire Convention and are considered inaccurate in some respects.

during the nineteenth and even in the twentieth century.[131] The most complete and most valuable of these are the notes of Madison, first published in 1840 and republished in various editions[132] as well as in several of the collections noted below. Madison's notes have in effect been accorded the status of an official report of the debates.[133]

The standard and invaluable source for the proceedings and debates of the Philadelphia convention is Max Farrand, ed., The Records of the Federal Convention of 1787. Originally issued in 1911 and revised in 1937,[134] this compilation is a day-by-day record of the Convention, giving for each day the text of all then available contemporary records[135] including the Convention journal and the notes

131. John Lansing's notes, covering only the first part of the Convention but containing some details not in other accounts, were rediscovered in 1901 and first published in 1939. Joseph Reese Strayer, ed., The Delegate from New York; or, Proceedings of the Federal Convention of 1787, from the notes of John Lansing, Jr. (Princeton U. and Oxford U. Press, 1939). For records first published in the late nineteenth and early twentieth centuries see Charles Warren, The Making of the Constitution, 803-04 (rev. ed., Little, Brown, 1937).

132. For a recent edition see Notes of Debates in the Federal Convention of 1787, reported by James Madison, with an introduction by Adrienne Koch (Athens, Ohio U. Press, 1966).

133. An early illustration is the Supreme Court's reference to the notes in Carpenter v. Pennsylvania, 58 U.S. (17 How.) 456, 463 (1855). For an account of Madison's labor as "unofficial secretary" of the Convention and an appraisal of his notes, see Rossiter, supra note 123, at 162-63.

134. 4 v., rev. ed. Yale U. Press, 1937, reprinted 1966.

135. Farrand did not include some material newly discovered but not then available, i.e., Lansing's notes and some papers of Charles Cotesworth Pinckney.

of Yates, Madison, King, and other delegates. Following this chronological account, and keyed thereto by footnotes, is a collection of pertinent supplementary materials including various draft proposals, excerpts from The Federalist, correspondence and other papers of the delegates, speeches in the state conventions, and Congressional debates in the early years of the nation. The entire collection is indexed both by clauses of the Constitution and by topic. Much of the same material, in less convenient arrangement, was published by the federal government in two earlier compilations.[136]

The debates in the various state conventions on ratification of the Constitution have apparently never been given the judicial deference accorded to The Federalist or the proceedings of the federal convention.[137] But they have nevertheless been referred to by the Supreme Court from time to time in construing the Constitution.[138] These

136. Charles C. Tansill, comp., Documents Illustrative of the Formation of the Union of the American States, was published by the Library of Congress in 1927, and was also issued as H.R. Doc. No. 398, 69th Cong., 1st Sess. A Documentary History of the Constitution of the United States was published in five volumes by the Department of State (1894-1905), reprinted in 1965 by Johnson Reprint Corp.

137. Compare Madison's repeated statement that the state conventions, and not the Philadelphia convention, constituted the authoritative source for the intent of the Constitution. Warren, *supra* note 131, at 793-94, 800-01. But Madison actually made numerous references to the Philadelphia proceedings in support of his own views. See Donald O. Dewey, James Madison Helps Clio Interpret the Constitution, 15 Am. J. Legal Hist. 38 (1971).

138. Mr. Justice Story in effect took judicial notice of the debates in the state conventions as well as statements made elsewhere at the time in Martin v. Hunter's Lessee, 14

debates were published, in part, in contemporary newspapers and later in separate books covering the respective conventions and varying considerably in completeness and accuracy. Since 1830, the most frequently used source for the state convention debates has been the compilation known as Elliot's Debates.[139] That work, however, was neither complete nor textually accurate, and in the intervening years additional records of the debates have been discovered.[140] Presently in progress under the auspices of the National Historical Publications Commission is the compilation of a complete documentary history of the ratification of the Constitution and the Bill of Rights. The first series of this project, when completed, will make available in one collection all known official and unofficial records of official action on ratification of the 1789 Constitution as well as public and private records of contemporary opinion.

U.S. (1 Wheat.) 304, 351 (1816). For extensive use of the state as well as the federal convention debates in a late nineteenth century case see the important opinion in Pollock v. Farmers Loan & Trust Co., 157 U.S. 429, 562-68 (1895).

139. Jonathan Elliot, ed., The Debates, Resolutions, and Other Proceedings, in Convention, on the Adoption of the Federal Constitution, as Recommended by the General Convention at Philadelphia, on the 17th of September, 1787: with the yeas and nays on the decision of the main question. Coll. and rev. from contemporary publications (4 v., Washington, 1827-30). This compilation appeared in several later editions with additions including Madison's notes of the debates in the Philadelphia convention and in the Continental Congress. It was reprinted in 5 volumes in 1937.

140. For a nineteenth-century supplementation of Elliot's Debates with respect to the ratification proceedings in Pennsylvania see John B. McMaster and Frederick D. Stone, Pennsylvania and the Federal Constitution 1787-1788 (originally published by the Historical Society of Pennsylvania in 1888; reprinted, 2 v., Da Capo Press, 1970).

A valuable guide to the legislative and other history of particular provisions of the 1789 Constitution is a volume by Edward Dumbauld, The Constitution of the United States (U. of Okla. Press, 1964). For each clause of the Constitution there are noted its origin and evolution in the Philadelphia convention (based principally upon and citing the appropriate passages in Farrand's Records), its antecedents in the Articles of Confederation or in English and colonial constitutional and legal history, its interpretation by the Supreme Court, and other interpretations subsequent to the convention including some references to the proceedings in the state conventions.

B. The Bill of Rights (1791)

To a large extent the 1789 Constitution was ratified on the understanding that a bill of rights would be added. Hence the legislative history of the first ten amendments involves in part the history of the formulation and adoption of the original Constitution. This includes the proposals for a bill of rights which had been rejected in the Philadelphia convention and in the Continental Congress during consideration of the convention report, The Federalist and other private writings during the struggle for ratification, and the recommendations made in the state conventions preceding ratification of the original Constitution. That legislative history continues with (a) the proceedings in the first session of Congress, beginning with Madison's introduction in the House of numerous proposed amendments to the body of the Constitution in June 1789 and ending with Congress' proposal in September 1789 of twelve articles to be appended to the Constitution, and (b) subsequent consideration by the state legislatures culminating in December 1791 with the ratification of ten of those amendments. There was also argumentative writing in the public press during this period.[141]

It is a curious fact that until recently no single publication attempted to collect all the relevant materials on the Bill of Rights. Bernard Schwartz, The Bill of Rights: A Documentary History (2 v., Chelsea House and McGraw Hill, 1971), reproduces, with commentary, the text of official federal and state records, private records and correspondence, and extracts from contemporary newspapers with respect to the legislative history of the Bill of Rights from the Philadelphia convention to ratification. It also contains the text of English and colonial antecedents, Revolutionary declarations and constitutions, and pertinent materials from the period of the Confederation. The National Historical Publications Commission project mentioned above will include so far as possible all official and unofficial records of

141. See Charles Warren, New Light on the History of the Federal Judiciary Act of 1789, 37 Harv. L. Rev. 49, 116, 121 (1923).

official action on the Bill of Rights as well as public and private records of contemporary comment.

For the legislative history materials prior to 1789, of course, the same sources may be utilized as those noted for the 1789 Constitution. For the proceedings in the first session of Congress, the basic sources are the first volume of the Annals of Congress, and -- for those having access to the few libraries which have copies -- the Senate and House Journals for that session.[142] Pertinent provisions from these records are reproduced in the Schwartz compilation. As the Senate debates in that Congress were secret, information as to the arguments in the Senate is obtainable only from private records and other papers of members of the Congress. In a recent case the Supreme Court cited for this purpose contemporary letters written by Madison, noting that William Maclay's journal does not cover the period during which the Senate discussed the proposals.[143]

142. Those portions of 1 Annals pertaining to the Bill of Rights are also reprinted in Bennett B. Patterson, The Forgotten Ninth Amendment, 93 et seq. (Bobbs-Merrill Co., 1955), but without indication of the original page numbers. The major portion of the House debates is also excerpted in Charles S. Hyneman and George W. Carey, A Second Federalist, ch. 11 (Appleton-Century-Crofts, 1967).

143. Williams v. Florida, 399 U.S. 78, 94-96 (1970). The most complete edition thus far published of Madison's writings is Gaillard Hunt, ed., Writings of James Madison (9 v., New York, G. P. Putnam's Sons, 1900-10). Now in course of publication, but not as yet covering the period of the adoption of the Constitution and the Bill of Rights, is Papers of James Madison (U. of Chicago Press, 1962-   ), edited by William T. Hutchinson and William M. E. Rachal. This collection, published under the sponsorship of the University of Chicago and the University of Virginia, will include much material previously unpublished and should supersede all prior editions.

There also exist in the National Archives and in the Rare Book Room of the Library of Congress manuscript and printed versions of the draft proposals for a bill of rights as they existed at various stages of Congressional consideration, which differ in some respects from the records as appearing in the Annals.[144]

Excellent detailed accounts of the adoption of the Bill of Rights appear in the following: Edward Dumbauld, The Bill of Rights and What It Means Today (U. of Okla. Press, 1957), which also contains an article-by-article summary of its genesis and a table indicating the sources of each provision and the stages of legislative history at which major changes were made as well as an extensive section on judicial interpretation; Robert Allen Rutland, The Birth of the Bill of Rights 1776-1791 (U. of N.C. Press, 1955), which also covers English, colonial, and Confederation history; and Charles Warren, New Light on the History of the Federal Judiciary Act of 1789, 37 Harv. L. Rev. 49 (1923), which places the legislative history of that statute in the context of the contemporary and related adoption of the Bill of Rights. A classic older but still valuable work is

---

144. See Edward Dumbauld, The Bill of Rights and What It Means Today, ix, 34 n.6 (U. of Okla. Press, 1957). This book reproduces from the Library of Congress prints the proposals as reported by the House Select Committee, as passed by the House, and as passed by the Senate. Other copies of the first two of these were published in volume 5 of the Documentary History compiled by the State Department, supra note 136, which also contains a few pertinent contemporary letters by Madison and others.

Francis Newton Thorpe, The Constitutional History of the United States 1765-1895 (3 v., Callaghan & Co., 1901, reprinted by Da Capo Press 1970). There are also several works useful with respect to the legislative history of particular amendments.[145]

The Bill of Rights, like all subsequent amendments except the Twenty-first, was ratified -- as the Constitution permits -- by the state legislatures rather than by state conventions. The resolutions and acts of the state legislatures from 1789 to 1791 ratifying all or some of the twelve amendments submitted to them by the first Congress are reproduced in the Schwartz compilation as well as in volume 2 of the Documentary History published by the State Department[146] and the second and third volumes of Annals of Congress. Information as to the debates in the state legislatures is sparse and fragmentary; some contemporary press accounts as well as pertinent messages of governors and correspondence are reproduced in the Schwartz compilation. As to a particular state, some data respecting the ratification process (al-

145. E.g., on the First Amendment, with special reference to the religion clauses: Anson P. Stokes and Leo Pfeffer, Church and State in the United States (rev. ed., Harper & Row, 1964), reproducing text of the House debates and excerpts from the Senate Journal; Leo Pfeffer, Church, State and Freedom (rev. ed., Beacon Press, 1967), also covering the Fourteenth Amendment and the unsuccessful Blaine amendment of 1875-76. On the Fourth Amendment: Nelson P. Lasson, The History and Development of the Fourth Amendment to the United States Constitution (Johns Hopkins Press, 1937). On the Sixth Amendment: Francis H. Heller, The Sixth Amendment to the Constitution of the United States (U. of Kans. Press, 1951). On the Ninth Amendment: Bennett P. Patterson, The Forgotten Ninth Amendment (Bobbs-Merrill Co., 1955).

146. Supra note 136.

though not the debates) will also be found in its legislative journals and public document collections, or in some instances in special studies.[147]

C. Subsequent Amendments and Proposals

Article V of the Constitution provides two methods by which amendments may be proposed, that is, either by Congress when deemed necessary by two-thirds of both houses or by a convention which Congress must call on application of the legislatures of two-thirds of the states. In either case, Congress may determine whether the requisite ratification by three-fourths of the states is to be by the state legislatures or by state conventions. All amendments submitted to the states thus far have been proposed by Congress;[148] and except for the Twenty-first Amendment repeal-

147. For a brief account of the controversies which delayed Virginia's ratification and prevented ratification by three other states at that time, see Irving Brant, The Bill of Rights: Its Origin and Meaning (Bobbs-Merrill Co., 1965). Pertinent contemporary letters of Madison and others respecting action in the Virginia legislature are quoted in Thorpe, Constitutional History, supra note 123, II, 261-63. For data respecting failure of the Massachusetts legislature to ratify at that time see Denys P. Myers, Massachusetts and the First Ten Amendments to the Constitution, S. Doc. No. 181, 74th Cong., 2d Sess. (1936). Connecticut, Georgia, and Massachusetts ratified the first ten Amendments in 1939.

148. Over the years there have been several movements to require Congress to call a convention, none thus far successful. See S. Doc. No. 91-38, note 150 infra, at vi-vii, and Ames, note 151 infra, at 281-84. A listing of requests made to Congress by state legislatures, with citations to the Congressional Record or other sources, appears in Cyril F. Brickfield, State Applications Asking Congress to Call a Federal Constitutional Convention, published as a committee print by the House Judiciary Committee, 87th Cong., 1st Sess. (1961).

ing national prohibition, Congress has invariably provided for ratification by the state legislatures. By 1969 nearly 7,000 resolutions for proposing constitutional amendments had been introduced in Congress; many of these, of course, embodied the same or similar proposals. The majority died in committee although others reached the stage of hearings, committee reports, or even debate and vote in one or both houses before defeat. Some were acted upon only after repeated reintroduction in successive Congresses. Only five have been submitted to but not ratified by the states, not including the recently submitted Women's Rights Amendment.

With respect to any such proposal, the legislative history materials relating to its handling by Congress are the same as those comprising the legislative history of a federal statute.[149] The method of locating them would be essentially the same were it not for some special research aids. Several works vastly simplify the task. For the period from 1927 through 1968, two compilations prepared by the Senate Library together list and index all such proposals introduced in Congress and indicate subsequent Congressional

149. Presidential approval is not required for Congress' proposal of constitutional amendments. Presidential messages recommending initiation of a proposal in Congress, however, are sometimes important elements in the legislative history.

action on each.[150] Separate legislative history tables, covering all proposals reaching hearing or later stages, furnish references to hearings available in the Senate Library, committee reports, debates, and votes in both houses. For all ratified amendments through the Twenty-fifth, the text and historical annotations are supplied. Three earlier works together provide detailed histories, though differing in scope and arrangement, for the period from 1789 through 1929.[151]

Accounts of the background and enactment process of the ratified amendments, and data concerning important unsuccessful proposals, are contained in the standard works on American constitutional history.[152] With respect to

---

150. Proposed Amendments to the Constitution of the United States of America Introduced in Congress from the 69th Congress, 2d Session through the 87th Congress, 2d Session, S. Doc. No. 163, 87th Cong., 2d Sess. (1963), and Proposed Amendments to the Constitution of the United States of America Introduced in Congress from the 88th Congress, 1st Session, through the 90th Congress, 2d Session, S. Doc. No. 91-38 (1969).

151. Herman V. Ames, The Proposed Amendments to the Constitution of the United States during the First Century of its History, 1896 Am. Hist. Ass'n Ann. Rep., II, also published as H.R. Doc. No. 353, Pt. 2, 54th Cong., 2d Sess., a detailed topical study covering also amendments proposed to Congress by state legislatures; Charles C. Tansill, Proposed Amendments to the Constitution of the United States, S. Doc. No. 93, 69th Cong., 1st Sess. (1926), covering 1890-1926; and M. A. Musmanno, Proposed Amendments to the Constitution, H.R. Doc. No. 551, 70th Cong., 2d Sess. (1929), a monograph covering 1890-1929 and also reviewing briefly prior proposed amendments covering subjects treated in amendments proposed during the principal period.

152. Amendments through the Twenty-first and Twenty-second, for example, are covered respectively in Andrew C. McLaughlin, Constitutional History of the United States (Appleton-Century-Crofts, 1935), and Carl Brent Swisher,

particular amendments there are also works providing more detailed legislative history, either in narrative form with reference to documentary sources, or in some cases reproducing the text of pertinent materials. Some particularly useful works of this nature are as follows:

Thirteenth and Fourteenth Amendments: Jacobus tenBroek, The Antislavery Origins of the Fourteenth Amendment (U. of Calif. Press, 1951), rev. ed. as Equal under Law (Collier Books, 1965).

Fourteenth Amendment: Charles Fairman and Stanley Morrison, The Fourteenth Amendment and the Bill of Rights: The Incorporation Theory (Da Capo Press, 1970.)[153] In addition to examination of the proceedings in Congress leading to proposal of the Amendment, this work covers in detail the proceedings in the state legislatures resulting in ratification (and in some instances subsequent state legislative action as contemporaneous construction of the Amendment) with

American Constitutional Development (2d ed., Houghton Mifflin Co., 1954). An older but still valuable history covering amendments through the Fifteenth is Francis Newton Thorpe, Constitutional History of the United States 1765-1895 (3 v., Callaghan & Co., 1901, reprinted, Da Capo Press, 1970).

153. This book reprints, with an introduction by Leonard W. Levy, two articles by Messrs. Fairman and Morrison originally published in 2 Stanford L. Rev. 5 and 140 (1949), in which they took issue with the theory that the Amendment "incorporated" or made applicable to the states the entire Bill of Rights, as expounded by Justice Black in his dissenting opinion in Adamson v. California, 332 U.S. 46, 68 (1947). Justice Black had drawn heavily on the Congressional history of the Amendment; Mr. Fairman's article focused primarily on the legislative history but reached the opposite conclusion. In his dissenting opinion some twenty years later in Duncan v. Louisiana, 391 U.S. 145, 174-75 (1968), Justice Harlan stated he was convinced by the historical evidence marshaled by Mr. Fairman; Justice Black, however, remained unconvinced. Id. at 165 (concurring opinion).

all available explanations including excerpts from and references to governors' messages, committee reports, and vote figures (and debates in Pennsylvania, the one state legislature reporting them). See also Benjamin B. Kendrick, ed., Journal of the Joint Committee of Fifteen on Reconstruction (Ph.D. dissertation, Columbia U., 1914), reproducing the journal of the joint committee of Congress on Reconstruction, 1865-67, relating principally to the genesis of the Fourteenth Amendment. Horace Edgar Flack, The Adoption of the Fourteenth Amendment (first published 1908; reprinted, Gloucester, Mass., P. Smith, 1965). Joseph B. James, The Framing of the Fourteenth Amendment (37 Ill. Studies in the Social Sciences, U. of Ill. Press, 1956).

Fifteenth Amendment: John M. Mathews, Legislative and Judicial History of the Fifteenth Amendment (first published 1909 as Johns Hopkins U. Studies in Hist. & Pol. Science, ser. 27, nos. 6-7; reprinted, Da Capo Press, 1971). William Gillette, The Right to Vote: Politics and the Passage of the Fifteenth Amendment, Johns Hopkins U. Studies in Hist. & Pol. Science, ser. 83, no. 1 (Johns Hopkins Press, 1965).

Sixteenth Amendment: U.S. Department of Justice, The Sixteenth Amendment: A Compilation of Extracts from Messages of the Governors and Other Material Contained in Legislative Journals (1938). U.S. Department of Justice, Taxation of Government Bondholders and Employees (1939). Part II of the latter publication contains detailed accounts of the proceedings in Congress and the state legislatures with references to official sources.

Twenty-first Amendment: Everett S. Brown, comp., Ratification of the Twenty-first Amendment to the Constitution of the United States (Ann Arbor, 1938, reprinted, Da Capo Press, 1970) reproduces from official sources the records of the state conventions as well as the statutes providing for the conventions.

PART VII

USABLE BACKGROUND FOR TREATY INTERPRETATION

Treaties are laws or, in the semantics of courts, are sometimes said to have the "effect" of laws. The Constitution lists them along with itself and other federal laws as subject to the judicial power and in the same fashion declares them to be a part of "the supreme law of the land."[154] But the legislative process for their making differs greatly and in critical respects from that of statute making. More than one government is involved -- at least two truly independent sovereign countries -- so that there is an element of mutuality or consensual agreement about them. They are initiated exclusively by the Executive and require the concurrence of only one house of Congress, the Senate by a two-thirds vote.[155] This background produces some documentary materials useful in the reading and interpretation of treaties.

Where documentation is available, negotiations culminating in a treaty may be used in its interpretation. Courts of the United States make use of such materials in the same way that the legislative history of a statute is

---

154. Art. III, § 2, and Art. VI.

155. U.S. Const., Art. II, § 2.

used in its interpretation.[156] These materials (called <u>travaux préparatoires</u>, or preparatory work, in the language of international law) have long been used for the same purposes by international courts and arbitral tribunals.[157] The Vienna Convention on the Law of Treaties, opened for signature in 1969 and presently awaiting accession by the requisite number of states, provides that preparatory work may be used as a supplementary means of interpretation but subject to certain limitations.[158] Joint statements made by negotiators or plenipotentiaries at the time of conclusion of a treaty, and unilateral statements at least when communicated to the other party or parties, are also proper

156. See, e.g., use of such materials from State Department and Congressional records and publications in the interpretation of bilateral treaties in Cook v. United States, 288 U.S. 102, 116-18 (1933); Nielsen v. Johnson, 279 U.S. 47, 52-55 (1929); United States v. Texas, 162 U.S. 1, 23-28 (1896). For use of proceedings of international conferences and commissions in construction of a multilateral convention see United States v. Louisiana, 394 U.S. 11 (1969). See also Restatement (Second) of Foreign Relations Law of the United States, § 147(d) (1965).

157. See L. Oppenheim, International Law, I, 957-58 (8th ed. H. Lauterpacht; London, Longmans, Green & Co., 1955); Arnold D. McNair, Law of Treaties, ch. 23 (Oxford, Clarendon Press, 1961); D. P. O'Connell, International Law, I, 262-64 (2d ed., London, Stevens & Sons, 1970); but see Myres S. McDougal and others, Interpretation of Agreements and World Public Order, 122-32 (Yale U. Press, 1967); Georg Schwarzenberger, International Law, I, 514-15 (3d ed., London, Stevens & Sons, 1957-68).

158. Art. 32, 8 Int'l Legal Materials 679, 692 (1969). For the view that this provision of the Convention will not alter the established practice of "discriminating recourse" to preparatory work see Herbert W. Briggs, The Travaux Préparatoires of the Vienna Convention on the Law of Treaties, 65 Am J. Int'l L. 705, 712 (1971).

sources of interpretation.[159] The consent proceedings in the United States Senate, while not a component of the preparatory work, may be useful as evidencing contemporaneous interpretation of a treaty by the United States; and Senate proceedings in rejecting a treaty may be important source material respecting a later treaty to which the Senate consented.[160]

Because the negotiation process, and consequently the documentation, differ with different types of treaties, it is difficult to summarize or suggest a settled research routine. However, in two situations valuable background material of an official nature is produced. One is in the formulation of multilateral conventions, that is, treaties in the making of which many nations participate and hence require meetings, discussions, and written communications of a public nature. The other is in the domestic process of Senate consent to ratification of any treaty, which requires communication between the Executive and the Senate and entails Senate committee reports and debates or other proceedings. In still a third situation, that of tax treaties, there are valuable supplemental sources of legislative history.

---

159. See Restatement (Second) of Foreign Relations Law of the United States, § 147(e) (1965); Charles C. Hyde, International Law, II, 1497-98 (2d rev. ed., Little, Brown, 1945).

160. See Lauterpacht, Some Observations on Preparatory Work in the Interpretation of Treaties, 48 Harv. L. Rev. 549, 575 (1935).

The available source materials covering the process of negotiating bilateral treaties are few and fragmentary. Such treaties are ordinarily negotiated with representatives of the other nation by representatives of the Department of State, frequently with the assistance of other executive departments and sometimes with advice from interested private groups. There is normally no formal record of the negotiation process except to the extent that it may appear in diplomatic papers published many years later.[161] General statements respecting the negotiations are frequently released by the Department at the time a treaty is concluded and occasionally during the course of negotiations. Sometimes a joint communiqué is issued on behalf of both parties. These statements are published in the weekly Department of State Bulletin. Some are reproduced in other compilations such as Documents on American Foreign Relations, published annually by the Council on Foreign Relations. More detailed statements respecting the negotiations occasionally appear in the hearings before the Senate committee as described below.

---

161. The standard source for American diplomatic papers beginning in 1861 is the State Department compilation presently entitled Foreign Relations of the United States, the latest volume of which usually contains records twenty to twenty-five years old. For the period beginning in 1925 this compilation contains materials relating to the negotiation of treaties, including intradepartmental memoranda as well as diplomatic correspondence, documents, and proceedings of a number of multilateral conferences and commissions.

Although foreign sources are not within the scope of this manual, it should be noted that records and unilateral statements of the other parties to a treaty, where available, may also be utilized as source material relating to the negotiation process.

Multilateral conventions, unlike bilateral treaties, are drawn up, perfected, and finally agreed to by one or a series of international groups, frequently large in number. Upon agreement by the last body in the series, the convention is ripe for signature and ratification by the nations represented in that body (and frequently by other nations). Some such conventions are originally conceived by unofficial international organizations and later considered and approved by bodies consisting of official representatives of the countries involved. Many, however, are entirely the product of international bodies having some official connection with the individual governments involved. Since World War II there has been a proliferation of international organizations concerned with the preparation of conventions, some regional and others worldwide. Many of these have been organs, creatures of, or organizations related to the United Nations, while others have had no connection with the United Nations. The proceedings of many, but by no means all, such groups are formally recorded and eventually published at least in summary form. It is these travaux preparatoires of multilateral conventions, therefore, which are most commonly utilized in treaty interpretation. An illustration of sources and research methods respecting one type of multilateral conventions follows.

A. Conventions Sponsored by the United Nations

For multilateral conventions concluded under the auspices of the United Nations, the principal legislative history materials are published as public records. The same is true of some, but not all, such conventions sponsored by the fourteen "specialized agencies." These are intergovernmental organizations related to, but independent of, the United Nations. To the extent that such source materials of the specialized agencies are officially published, they will appear in the publications of the individual agency. Examples are the proceedings and reports of the International Labor Conference of the International Labor Organization with respect to numerous labor conventions.

The processes. But even as to conventions sponsored by the United Nations proper, these source materials are not to be found in any single series of U.N. publications. A variety of methods, involving a variety of bodies, have been used for their preparation and approval. Some have been drafted and opened for signature by an international conference specially convened for that purpose pursuant to resolution of the General Assembly or of one of its principal organs. Some have been drafted, considered, and agreed to by a special committee of the United Nations and thereafter considered and approved by the General Assembly. Some have been first considered by a unit of one of the principal U.N. organs such as a commission of the Economic and Social Council, then by the full body of that organ, and finally by the General Assembly.

With respect to several conventions designed to "codify" international law, a three-step procedure has been followed: (1) The first is consideration of the subject by the International Law Commission, either on its own initiative or at the request of the General Assembly, including the preparation and revision of drafts. This may extend over a period of several sessions during which time one or more drafts may be submitted to member governments for comment. It culminates in submission of a final draft to the General Assembly with recommendation for the convening of an international conference. (2) Next is consideration in the General Assembly -- first by a committee and later in plenary session -- culminating in the adoption of a resolution directing the convening of an international conference to which the Commission draft will be referred as a basic proposal. (3) There follow consideration and revision by such a conference, sometimes first in committee and later in plenary session, culminating in final approval of the convention and its opening for signature. Steps (1) and (2) not infrequently overlap to some extent since the General Assembly or one of its committees may give active consideration to a Commission draft before it reaches final form. At various stages valuable commentaries and guides may be prepared by the U.N. Secretariat for the use of the body then considering the proposal. Conventions adopted following this general procedure include among others those respecting the Law of the Sea and the Law of Treaties.

Preliminary search. The first requisite in a search for the preparatory work of a multilateral convention concluded under the aegis of the United Nations is a history of the process by which it came into being. This may be a skeletonized history but should indicate which organs of the United Nations participated in the process and at what time or times. Frequently such information can most easily be obtained in the scholarly literature of international law, particularly as to proceedings of recent date. With respect to any convention of major importance, articles and even books will appear shortly after its adoption if not earlier during protracted stages of its development. These invariably outline the history with documentary references. Often proposals and arguments made at various stages in U.N. organs and conferences are analyzed in depth.

The source material of a particular U.N.-sponsored convention may also be identified by reference to one or more U.N. publications. A most valuable guide is the Yearbook of the United Nations, published by the U.N. Office of

Public Information. As to each proposed convention on which some action was taken or recommended during the year by any unit of the United Nations, the _Yearbook_ contains a summary of such action or recommendation with references to documents and proceedings. Frequently arguments and proposals are stated in detail and occasionally documents are quoted or reproduced in full. The _Yearbook_ also covers, but in less detail, activities of the specialized agencies. It is indexed alphabetically by subject as well as by organ. Unfortunately, its publication is habitually long delayed. An ample history is readily obtainable by consulting first the _Yearbook_ for the year in which a convention was concluded, if available, and then the earlier _Yearbooks_, in reverse chronological order, until the point of origin of the convention proposal is reached. If the convention was concluded after the latest year covered by the _Yearbook_, the most recent _Yearbooks_ available should first be consulted, after which the search may be supplemented by reference to one or more of the sources of current data noted below.

A supplementary or alternative source for skeleton histories is provided by the _United Nations Juridical Yearbook_ published for the years beginning 1962 by the U.N. Office of Legal Affairs. This work contains a "Legal Documents Index" of the United Nations and related organizations, arranged by organization and constituent unit. Current activities of each unit, grouped by subject matter under that unit, are outlined with references to documents and debates. A similar arrangement is used for a bibliographical section which follows. This Yearbook also reproduces the texts of selected recommendations and reports by the United Nations and related organizations as well as treaties concluded under their auspices.

There are also annual volumes covering developments in special fields, such as the Yearbook of the United Nations Commission on International Trade Law, first published in 1971 but covering from 1968.

Mention should also be made of Multilateral Treaties in Respect of Which the Secretary-General Performs Depositary Functions: List of Signatures, Ratifications, Accessions, etc., published by the U.N. Office of Legal Affairs and reissued as of the end of each calendar year. This publication lists all multilateral international agreements which designate the Secretary-General of the United Nations as depositary as well as instruments affecting earlier agreements the depositary functions under which were formerly performed by the League of Nations. It does not list all agreements filed or registered with the Secretariat, or even all agreements promulgated under the sponsorship of the United Nations. It does not, for example, list the Treaty on the Non-Proliferation of Nuclear Weapons (which provides for deposit of instruments of ratification and accession with the governments of the United States, Great Britain, and Russia) even though the proposal for that treaty originated in the U.N. General Assembly and that body considered it extensively and commended the final text. Within the scope of its coverage, however, it is a valuable tool. While its primary use is for references to ratifications, reservations, denunciations, etc., it also supplies for each convention listed one or more references which may be used as a starting point for legislative history search if more complete data are otherwise not readily available. For example, as to the conventions on the Law of the Sea, there are citations to the General Assembly resolution convening the Geneva Conference of 1958 and to the proceedings of that Conference, but not to the proceedings of the International Law Commission or to the proceedings of the General Assembly preceding the resolution. The dates and references furnished, however, afford a base from which the search may move backwards in time.

Marjorie M. Whiteman, ed., Digest of International Law, publication of which by the Department of State began in 1963, contains a very full history of a number of multilateral conventions, primarily those in the field of public international law. In addition to detailed coverage of the evolution of the conventions with references to and frequently quotations from relevant documents and proceedings, it relates the prior historical background including relevant proceedings of earlier official or unofficial bodies.

Since the work is topically arranged, the history of one provision of a particular convention may be separated from that of other provisions. Where the subject matter of a particular convention falls within a single topical subdivision, however, the history of that convention will be found in one place under that subdivision. This is the case, for example, in chapter 34, "Arms Control and Disarmament," appearing in volume 11 (published in 1968), which contains the history of the Limited Nuclear Test Ban Treaty of 1963, the Outer Space Treaty of 1967, and of the Non-Proliferation Treaty of 1968 as far as August 1967.

To obtain references to materials more recent than those covered in the available yearbooks and other publications described above, several official and unofficial guides are useful. The United Nations Monthly Chronicle, published by the U.N. Office of Public Information, summarizes current developments including the activities of international conferences as well as of the General Assembly committees and plenary sessions. Brief summaries of such activities are also contained in United Nations Law Reports, published monthly by the Walker Publishing Company. Listings of U.N. publications (but not, in recent years, publications of the specialized agencies) received by the U.N. Library during the period covered appear in the United Nations Documents Index, which is published in eleven issues per year plus an annual index and checklist. International Legal Materials, published bimonthly by the American Society of International Law, publishes the text of some important documents and notices of others. The weekly Department of State Bulletin contains information concerning recent developments with particular emphasis on the position taken by representatives of the United States, occasionally reproducing the text of their statements or reports. Press releases announcing recent activities, issued by the U.N. Office of Public Information, are available in some libraries.

Locating source materials. When information has been obtained as to which bodies of the United Nations considered the proposed convention and over what period of time, the next problem is that of locating the text of the proceedings and documents. If, for example, the skeleton history indicates a convention was concluded under the three-step process described above involving participation of the International Law Commission, it will be necessary to consult three different compilations for the appropriate periods, as follows:

The proceedings and documents comprising the first step -- the International Law Commission drafts -- are issued as publications of the International Law Commission. Customarily, these reports and other documents are first issued separately in mimeographed form. Later the proceedings and most of the documents are published in the Yearbook of the Commission. Each Yearbook is issued in two volumes, the first containing a summary record of the Commission's proceedings and the second the text of documents including its report to the General Assembly, drafts of proposed conventions, memoranda by its rapporteurs and by the U.N. Secretariat, formal position papers of governments, and so on. Some documents, such as working papers, are listed but not reproduced. Ready access to all materials on a given subject is provided for each volume of the Yearbook by either an index, a detailed table of contents, or both. Each report of the Commission to the General Assembly has also been reproduced in an early issue of the American Journal of International Law with the exception of the Commission's report of 1968, which was reproduced in volume 8 of International Legal Materials (1969).

The source materials resulting from the second step -- Assembly consideration -- are issued as publications of the General Assembly. Most of the reports and other documents are first made available in separate mimeographed form. Later several series of separate pamphlets or "fascicles" are published which together comprise the Official Records of the General Assembly for the particular session. These include summary records of the meetings of the General Assembly in plenary session and in committee, and "annexes" and serially numbered "supplements" containing the text of reports, resolutions, and other documents. Some documents, however, are not included. Documents in the annexes are grouped into fascicles by agenda item number, but each document retains and is identified by the classification number assigned it on original issuance. Beginning in 1950, the United Nations Library publishes an index to the Official Records for each session giving references by subject to discussions in committee as well as in plenary sessions by meeting number and to reports, resolutions, and other documents by document or supplement number.

Where International Law Commission action was requested by the General Assembly, of course, the Official Records are also a necessary source for General Assembly proceedings leading to such request. The text of a General Assembly resolution formally requesting the Commission to take action will appear both in the Commission's Yearbook and in the Official Records. The same is true of the Commission's reports to the General Assembly.

The source materials of the third step -- conference proceedings considering and approving the draft convention -- are published and separately classified as official records of the conference in question. An example is the United Nations Conference on the Law of Treaties. The format may include separate parts or volumes devoted to preparatory documents, committee proceedings, plenary meetings, and "annexes" of documents, with a detailed table of contents for each section or part but usually no general index.

There is routinely a lengthy delay between the occurrence of any United Nations action and the publication in final printed form of the documents and proceedings comprising that action. Most of the reports and other documents, however, appear in mimeographed form some time before the final prints are available. Many, although by no means all, of the mimeographed documents are released for general distribution and may be found in libraries subscribing thereto. Some documents, as indicated above, are reproduced in International Legal Materials or in other unofficial periodicals; and some are reproduced in official publications of interested states.

B. U.S. Senate Consent Proceedings

The material which follows is confined to those international agreements entered into by the United States which are subject to the advice and consent of the Senate.[162] This process begins either when the Executive has negotiated and signed a treaty with one or more other nations or when it determines that the United States should ratify or accede to a multilateral convention drawn under the auspices of the United Nations or other international body.[163] In either

---

162. Postal conventions and certain executive agreements are not considered subject to the constitutional requirement; their legislative history therefore ends with approval by the Executive.

163. There is sometimes a delay between the time a multilateral convention is approved by the drafting body and the date it is signed by the plenipotentiary of the United

case the President sends a message to the Senate transmitting the instrument for its advice and consent. It is accompanied by a report made to him by the Secretary of State and other papers. These materials are printed in a separate series of Congressional publications entitled Senate Executive Documents.

Each Executive Document consists of the materials comprising a single submittal, almost invariably relating to a single treaty. Treaties received by the Senate during each session of Congress are lettered serially in order of receipt, and the Executive Document relating to each treaty is designated by the same letter. Thus, the first treaty transmitted by the President to the Senate in 1967 would be designated Executive A, 90th Cong., 1st Sess., and would retain that designation so long as pending in the Senate; and the proposed treaty, President's message, and any accompanying papers would be printed together as Senate Executive Document A, 90th Cong., 1st Sess.

Formerly the Senate Executive Documents were printed as confidential documents. Since 1945 they have ordinarily been printed without that classification. Yet

States. There may also be a delay between the latter date and the date of transmittal to the Senate. The Vienna Convention on the Law of Treaties, for example, was opened for signature in May 1969, signed for the United States in April 1970, and transmitted by the President to the Senate in November 1971. The Convention on the Political Rights of Women, adopted in 1953 but not signed by the United States, was transmitted by the President to the Senate in 1963 for advice and consent as to accession and was still on the Senate committee's calendar in January 1972, having been tabled in 1967.

they are not distributed to depository libraries and are not widely available as such. The President's messages, however, are customarily printed in the Congressional Record shortly after their receipt as well as in the Weekly Compilation of Presidential Documents, and frequently in the Department of State Bulletin. The Secretary's reports are sometimes published in the hearings, as indicated below. A number have been reproduced in the "Contemporary Practice of the United States" section of the American Journal of International Law. A few have been included in State Department compilations of foreign policy documents. For example, several are reproduced in American Foreign Policy, 1950-1955: Basic Documents, State Dept. Publication No. 6446 (2 v., 1957). For those respecting tax treaties, see below.

All treaties transmitted by the President to the Senate are referred, with their accompanying papers, to the Senate Committee on Foreign Relations.[164] The Committee (or a subcommittee) may or may not hold hearings on the treaty. Hearings held may or may not be public. Many, but not all, of the public hearings as well as some of those held in executive session are printed and sooner or later made available in the same manner as other Congressional hearings. The published hearings invariably

---

164. For a study of the functions and procedures of that committee see David N. Farnsworth, The Senate Committee on Foreign Relations (U. of Ill. Press, 1961).

contain statements by representatives of the Department of State, which sometimes contain data respecting the negotiation process; and they sometimes reproduce the text of the report of the Secretary of State to the President. They may also contain important statements by representatives of other executive departments or agencies. Where a multilateral convention is involved, frequently documents and proceedings of the United Nations or other international bodies are reproduced or quoted in the hearings.

The committee may consider a treaty and report it favorably to the Senate as submitted, or it may recommend approval with an amendment or with the addition of a reservation or qualification. Although the committee could submit an unfavorable report, its customary practice is simply to take no formal action on a treaty unless and until it has decided to recommend that the Senate consent. Sometimes a committee vote to table is made a matter of public record. Since pending treaty submittals (unlike pending bills and resolutions) do not expire at the end of each Congress, there may be pending before the committee at any given time agreements submitted by the Executive many years earlier. The same is sometimes also the case as to submittals reported by the committee but not acted upon by the Senate.[165] On occasion, where action has been long

165. In January 1972 there were pending before the Senate three multilateral conventions transmitted to it by the President in 1949. The committee had taken no action respecting two of these. As to the third, the Convention

delayed, the President has renewed his request for advice and consent, in which case of course the second message and any available accompanying documents are also a part of the legislative history. The Executive may also request the Senate to return a proposal, and there have been instances when the Senate has solicited such a request.

The reports of the Senate Committee on Foreign Relations respecting treaties are published in a separate series entitled Senate Executive Reports. These reports, however, are not distributed to depository libraries and are not generally available. The reports from 1789 to 1901 were reproduced in eight volumes in S. Doc. No. 231, 56th Cong., 2d Sess. (1901). Some of the reports on multilateral conventions in recent years were printed in the Congressional Record at the time the conventions were considered on the floor of the Senate.[166] Selected reports are occasionally reproduced in compilations of foreign policy documents.[167] For the reports respecting tax treaties, see below.

---

on Prevention and Punishment of Genocide, the President in 1970 renewed his request and the committee thereafter twice submitted reports.

166. Thus the Executive Report on the Law of the Sea conventions was published in 106 Cong. Rec. 11189 (1960), and that on the Non-proliferation Treaty (including majority and minority reports) in 114 Cong. Rec. 29026 (1968).

167. A number of the reports are reproduced in American Foreign Policy, 1950-1955: Basic Documents, State Dept. Publication No. 6446 (2 v., 1957).

After the committee has made a favorable report to the Senate, the treaty comes before the full Senate for vote on a resolution of advice and consent. The proceedings may be in closed or open session. If it is considered in open session, the debates are published in the Congressional Record. If the resolution receives the required two-thirds vote, the treaty may then be ratified and proclaimed by the President. Any amendments made or reservations added by the Senate are subject to approval by the Executive; and of course amendments are also subject to acceptance by the other party or parties to the treaty. Occasionally, instead of proposing specific language, the Senate returns the treaty to the Executive for suggested changes.

The Presidential proclamation of a treaty incorporates the text of the ratified treaty. Each such document is currently published by the State Department as a separate pamphlet in a numbered series entitled Treaties and Other International Acts Series; the same materials are later republished in chronological order in permanent form in the compilation United States Treaties and Other International Agreements. Prior to 1950 these materials were published in the Statutes at Large. Proclamations respecting treaties, unlike other Presidential proclamations, are not published in the Federal Register or Code of Federal Regulations. They are noted in the current issues of the Weekly Compilation of Presidential Documents and the Department of State Bulletin.

The materials published in the Congressional Record respecting a treaty may be located through its general index for the session or sessions involved.[168] But the Congressional Record does not contain a chronology of the legislative history of treaties. The date of signature and the date the Senate advised ratification (but no intervening history) are stated in the proclamation and noted, with other pertinent data, preceding the text of the proclamation in the current treaty publications described above. For treaties pending before the Senate in recent years, the most complete listing of information respecting action in that body appears in the latest available issue for a particular session of the Calendar of the Senate Committee on Foreign Relations. It contains a cumulative list covering every treaty pending during the current session including those carried over from prior sessions as well as those transmitted by the President during that session. For each treaty, the list notes the date of every action taken by a subcommittee, the full committee, or the Senate from the date of reference to the committee to date, with citation to the relevant committee report. It also indicates whether hearings were public and whether they have been printed. Recent action may be traced through the bi-

---

168. The index sometimes lists these materials under the heading "Treaties" and not under an entry for the subject matter of the treaty.

weekly indexes to the Congressional Record and its Daily Digest as well as through some commercial reporting services. The Congressional Index service, published by Commerce Clearing House, contains a "Treaties" section giving for each treaty pending before the Senate during the current Congress the dates of hearings, reports, and Senate action. Brief abstracts of published hearings and of Executive Documents and Executive Reports appear in the Congressional Information Service publications, CIS/Annual and CIS/Index, described above. These documents are also listed in the Government Printing Office Monthly Catalog. Two publications of the Department of State provide references for the basic history of treaties submitted to the Senate prior to 1945. They are List of Treaties Submitted to the Senate, 1789-1934 (Publication 765), and Treaties Submitted to the Senate, 1935-1944 (Publication 2311).

C. Additional Sources for Tax Treaties

The United States is a party to a number of bilateral treaties relating to income, estate, and gift taxes. These agreements, customarily called tax conventions, are designed to avoid double taxation and to prevent tax evasion. The Departments of State and Treasury collaborate in negotiating them. When they are under consideration by the Senate Committee on Foreign Relations, assistance is furnished by representatives of the Treasury Department and the staff of the Joint Committee on Internal Revenue Taxation. Frequently detailed technical memoranda by Treasury or Joint Committee staff are printed in the hearings or as appendixes to the committee reports.

The post-negotiation legislative history materials of tax treaties are more readily available in convenient form than are the comparable materials for any other category of United States treaties. In 1962 the Joint Committee on Internal Revenue Taxation published a four-volume compilation entitled Legislative History of United States Tax Conventions. It covers all tax treaties to which the United States was then a signatory including treaties not then ratified as well as those in effect. For each treaty, the complete legislative history is reproduced, including the President's message to the Senate, the Secretary's report to the President, hearings if any, committee report, Senate debates, and proclamations. Also included are texts, commentaries, and related materials concerning model tax conventions prepared under the auspices of the League of Nations, the Organization for Economic Cooperation and Development, and other international organizations. The Tax Treaties service published by Commerce Clearing House, covering income and estate tax treaties in force and pending, reproduces the Secretary's and committee reports and pertinent releases, and furnishes current information as to matters in progress. The Cumulative Bulletin of the Internal Revenue Service occasionally reproduces major portions of the committee reports.

Index